MW01232887

Following the Ancient Paths:

An Unexpected Journey

by T. Durant Fleming, MDiv, DMin

Printed in the United States of America

ISBN 978-0-692-35110-9

St. Leopold Press
Memphis, Tennessee

Designed by Gloria C. White & Associates, Memphis, TN

Cover image: An ancient mosaic from the apse of the Basilica St. Paul Outside the Walls, located in Rome.

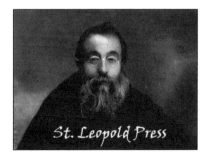

March 29, 2013

Good Friday

This is what the Lord says:
'Stand at the crossroads and look; ask for the ancient paths,
ask where the good way is, and walk in it,
and you will find rest for your souls.'

Jeremiah 6:16

This work is dedicated to my best friend and wife Sharon,
who, in the uniqueness of divine providence,
has been step for step my constant traveling companion
throughout this entire journey.

Following the Ancient Paths
Table of Contents

Foreword

A.M.D.G.

As a Christian Brother stationed in his home town—a rarity—I had the pleasure (and sometimes without the permission of my superior) of frequent visits with my parents at their home in Memphis. After my father's departure to heaven, I continued our Saturday lunches just with mother. Often in our conversations, my former students, Durant Fleming and his close friend Nick Bragorgos, were mentioned.

Durant, a Presbyterian minister with a doctorate in religious studies, expressed a genuine curiosity in teaching, church history, the founder of the Christian Brothers St. John Baptist de LaSalle, and Catholicism in general. During one of my visits home, my mother once remarked from her den chair about Durant, "That boy is going to become a Catholic!" We smiled and went about our visit. Today, more than a decade after Mother's prediction, you are holding in your hands the book that tells of this unexpected journey.

Following the Ancient Paths takes the reader by the heart and head and hand and creatively brings them on a pilgrimage, an earnest pilgrimage, which led him to an unforeseen place, the Catholic Church. In this refreshingly easy-to-read work, Durant opens his scrapbook, as it were, and shows the joys, the sorrows, the quandaries, and the revelations of a unique spiritual journey. In this concise work, we travel to faraway places, learn much about the history of the Church, and explore the beauty of faith. We meet, without names, friends, colleagues, and family who question, resent, accept, and embrace Durant's journey. In this short work, Durant paints with words the beauty, mystery, and wonder of a sincere journey of faith.

Just as Durant comes home to Christian Brothers High School as a leader and educator the summer of 2014, he also comes home to the Catholic Church in this treasured memoir.

Brother Joel William McGraw, F. S. C.
Christian Brothers High School, Memphis, Tennessee

Preface

One night late as I sat at my computer crafting this text, my daughter walked in and blurted in frustration, "There's no way I can cram everything I need for the next eleven months into this backpack!" She was preparing for an eleven-month mission trip, working in eleven different countries ranging climatically from Zambia to Mongolia, living the whole time out of a single backpack. I offered the simple, emotionally unsatisfying solution of a practical dad: "Pack less."

She scurried away, growling like one of the beasts she would soon encounter in the African bush. (Interestingly, after a few months in the field, she jettisoned even more and found genuine peace in simplicity.) I continued to type, listening to her and my Eagle Scout son as they re-packed her gear in earnest, leaving out a jacket, socks, some pricey tennis shoes, another couple of t-shirts, a fleece vest... As I listened to them debating over what really mattered, what genuinely needed to be included, I smiled. Little did my daughter know: I was facing the same dilemma at the same moment as I sat writing this book.

The task before me was to tell of a rich journey. It involved a sojourn, as you'll see, that spanned oceans, involved years of research, and called for a rigorous examination of evidence. Years of fascinating travel, dozens of rich interviews, hundreds of books read—how was I going to package all that? I heeded my own advice: "Pack less."

Just as my daughter—now a missionary in China as this is written—possesses only what she shoved into her backpack six months ago, I have attempted thoughtfully to incorporate into this book just the essential, seminal moments of a unique journey of faith.

Writing this manuscript was a solitary process, yet, it was not accomplished without the support and assistance of others. I would like to express my gratitude to Tom Dorian, who "made me" write this book. As I often chide him, this entire project is actually his fault. I thank Deacon Jeff Drzycimski for taking the time to read an early draft, then challenging me to give my wife a voice.

I would acknowledge the skilled editing work of David Yawn. Since I am absolutely certain that I do not possess a gift for editing, I am very grateful that David certainly does. It was a joy to work with such a professional on this book.

This endeavor could not exist without my wife and traveling partner Sharon, who was with me on this wonderful journey every step of the way. This is very much a shared story.

I must also express my sincere appreciation to my two sons, Carson and Jake, who unwittingly encouraged me every time they stopped by my office at home, asking what I was writing about at that moment. During these visits we had many lively and meaningful conversations about life. I shall always cherish those rich impromptu discussions.

Finally, let me thank my daughter Caroline, who has inspired us all to take those challenging steps of faith when God calls…and to pack less.

under A Spell?

How did a Presbyterian minister of twenty-five years become a devoted, practicing Catholic? Did he abandon all his Reformed theological training? Has he embraced some diluted form of the Gospel? Was he subtly be-spelled by the Catholic aesthetics of candles, incense, vestments, mystery, and icons? Was he somehow lured into the Catholic Church by the grace of folks who showed him special attention, knowing he'd be a "great catch"? Perhaps as a pastor he experienced some anguished church occurrence that soured him on Protestantism. Or possibly a tragic crisis of faith befell him, and like a drowning man began grasping at anything that he thought might bring him relief or security of soul.

I can assure you that none of these scenarios is at all close to the reality of the pilgrimage that led me into the full fellowship of the Catholic Church. It is the intent of this brief, informal work to faithfully dissect this curious transition—a transition not unique to me. Each chapter of this work represents about a year of my journey. Each page reflects months of reading, reflection, research, meditation, prayer, travel, interviews, and heartfelt dedication to ecclesiastic exploration. I was never passive in this endeavor. I learned as an undergraduate student in journalism that to get a story right you have to be patient, objective, relentless, thorough, accurate, and truthful. I have sincerely tried to be true to these journalistic principles. The following pages are my best efforts to accurately record this journey of faith.

Standing at the Reformation Wall, Geneva, Switzerland.

A Presbyterian's Presbyterian

Had you told me fifteen years ago that I would be writing a work on why I am a Catholic, I would have suggested you were jesting, or very odd, or outright insane. There would have been no other conceivable category.

Paul, in Philippians, recounts that, before his unforeseen conversion, he was a Jew among Jews, of the Tribe of Benjamin, a Pharisee's Pharisee, a dyed-in-the-wool Hebrew. He thumped his chest, touting his thorough Jewishness. In his mind, according to his plan, there was emphatically, certainly, absolutely no way he would ever become a lowly, scorned, persecuted Christian. God loves such challenges, I've learned. Had you hinted, years ago, that I would become a Catholic, I would have looked you squarely in the eyes—all the more dramatic were I wearing my severe, unadorned Presbyterian robe and my floppy John Calvin doctoral headgear—and proclaimed with certitude that, "I am a dedicated champion of Protestant theology. I have spent a good portion of my adult life earning a master's of divinity and a doctorate. For the love of decency, my dissertation research was in the realm of ecclesiology, the study of the Church. I have taught and preached thousands of lessons advancing the doctrines of Protestantism and the Presbyterian Church. I have made the pilgrimage to Geneva to study the life and teachings of John Calvin, John Knox and Ulricht Zwingli. In seminary I read John Calvin's, *Institutes of the Christian Religion* back-to-back, twice. I have journeyed to Edinburgh, the seat of Scottish Presbyterianism, where I've proudly stood before the National Covenant, a document signed in the blood of Protestant Scotsmen who freely gave their lives by the thousands for the cause during the Killing Times. I play the bagpipes, have a Scottish tartan doctoral hood, and love Harris tweed. No, I am a *Protestant*…and here I stand!" (That last was a Lutheran reference, if you missed it.)

So the question stands: How indeed does a seasoned minister with professionally honed theological sensibilities, one who's drafted and delivered a thousand worship services, married and buried hundreds of parishioners, taught Protestant theology and biblical studies at the high school, college, and graduate levels become a committed Catholic? The short answer: It has been one of the most marvelously challenging, socially curious, intellectually stimulating, career vexing, at times lonely, yet soul-gratifying experiences of my life.

Why Write This?

After almost a quarter of a century of service in a conservative, Reformation-oriented branch of the Presbyterian Church, I've made many wonderful and lasting friendships. These are people I love deeply. You have to understand, Scottish Presbyterianism is as loyal and tenacious as it gets. There is a good reason why kilted Scots wear a dagger in their stockings—it's to defend the clan, it is to protect your people. Next time you see someone in a kilt, look for it. They will have a dagger, called by Scots a *sgian dubh*, tucked neatly into a stocking or kilt hose. Not only do I understand this historically, but when I wear a kilt I, too, carry that dagger (though on the left side, being left-handed). The sgian dubh as a statement is about intense loyalty. I grasp that fierce Protestantism. It was forged in the furnace of a fiery history. I visited the place where the brave Scotswoman Janet Geddes, who, in protest, hurled a stool at the head of a clergyman during a service at St. Giles Cathedral and sparked a riot that launched the Scottish Reformation. Protestantism...I *get* it.

Why write this? Because I have prayed with my friends, taught them from the Scriptures, married them, visited them at the lowest points of their lives and mine, buried their parents, and celebrated life's joys together. I have helped to start new churches, served on mission trips, baptized a legion of pudgy children, stood by the gaping gravesides of relatives, belly-laughed and cried, shared sumptuous meals, danced in celebration at weddings, passionately hunted ducks, ridden loud motorcycles, eagerly traveled widely, savored the finest Scotch, and shared life deeply with my dear friends. The last thing I want to do is to confuse these friends or, worse yet, discourage someone in their own journey of faith.

This book was *not* written, please be clear, to prove anyone wrong. Rather, this short written effort may help someone to understand better.

One of my favorite early Church fathers was Irenaeus, the "lover of peace." Irenaeus believed that if we truly love one another, issues of discovering truth together are never to be framed in the language of victory and defeat. Following truth is a sojourn. There may be others who are feeling a peculiar tug, a gentle, unrelenting, deep and mysterious undertow. They are quietly seeking more, asking hard questions, thirsting for something about the faith they can't quite pinpoint. Some have quietly considered investigating the Catholic Church. This work is also dedicated to helping those pilgrims, who may be beginning their own journeys along the ancient paths, to find their way home. As my wise and ever-patient father used to say when facing a mystery, "You just never know."

There is another potentially helpful application of this work that only came to light in the midst of its writing. As I began in earnest to interview Catholics about their beliefs, I quickly learned that priests were historically and theologically very self-aware and could handle all types of questions. They know their stuff. During my research, I visited Rome and spent precious time with priests studying for their doctorates at the Pontifical North American College—a rich time of earnest dialogue and discovery. One night in Rome, I had the wonderful opportunity to enjoy a splendid dinner of artichokes, ravioli, red wine, and fresh bread with priests who were finishing their studies, just emerging from the academic trenches. They were gracious, exceedingly helpful, and thoroughly engaging in our discussions. Our dinner talk was as delicious as the food that night. Yet in my study of Catholicism I had noticed a precipitous drop in ecclesiastical and theological knowledge when I stepped outside the circle of clergy and began to speak with laity. (No great surprise—one finds the same in the Protestant world). I remember one evening at a dinner party listening to a proud cradle Catholic holding forth. He busied himself, with quite some zeal, misrepresenting a key Catholic doctrine. Upon hearing this, my wife sent me a curious look across the room and I mouthed the words, "We'll talk later." Surprisingly, I found that many cradle Catholics did not know what they believed, or, no less important, why they believed it. The Catholic tradition being so immensely rich—it is an endless buffet of amazing history, exquisite art, well-honed theology, inspiring biographies, and profound ideas—I was curious why more laypeople were not feasting at the banquet. Yet, as a counter-balance to this observation, I have also noticed a growing, enthusiastic interest by many Catholics to learn more about their faith and explore the deep spiritual wealth of their heritage.

Thus this work might be helpful to Catholic parishioners as well, offering them a ring-side seat to a Protestant seeking to understand and wind his way through some of the history, ideas, and common misunderstandings regarding the Catholic Church.

Though at times this journey felt lonely, it was definitely not a solo expedition. My wife Sharon was with me the whole way. In

preparing this manuscript, I had a theologian examine it and, after his thorough reading, we met for a memorable conversation. At one point he asked, "Where was your wife in this migration toward Catholicism? What did she think about all this? You mention her occasionally," he said, "but I was curious about her perspective. While you were involved in these rich theological and historical explorations, what, as a pastor's

Sharon and I celebrate graduation from my doctoral program.

wife of more than two decades, was she thinking? Certainly, Sharon had an opinion." Indeed she did. We had traveled this curious path together.

Sharon and I had met in our twenties at a Presbyterian Bible study. We were married in the Presbyterian Church, and while in seminary, we worked together to help start two new Presbyterian churches. Sharon was present when church elders laid hands upon me at my ordination service, and she held each of our three children as they were baptized at a Presbyterian church. She has patiently attended hundreds and hundreds of Presbyterian worship services. I had uprooted Sharon from her hometown and transplanted her three different times, following my studies and denominational duties. I had asked her to endure the significant financial struggles that accompany life in seminary in a distant city. I had pulled her away from friends with each move. She had faithfully endured my doctoral program while raising three small children, and I had asked her to sacrifice countless evenings and weekends to weddings, funerals, hospital visits, conferences, speaking engagements, and services all across the

South. She was a tough pastor's wife and a thorough-going Presbyterian. So what did Sharon think about becoming a Catholic? You will find out as you read this manuscript.

After finishing a draft of this book, I handed Sharon a printed copy and asked her, wherever she wanted within the text, to inject her thoughts and feelings about her journey into the Catholic Church. It was, after all, no less her story than mine. I encouraged her to write whatever she wanted to write. Initially she balked, saying, "You have the theological degrees, you are the student of church history, and you *like* to write!" But after some time, I coaxed her to tell some of her story as well. This was important to me. Without her part, it could never be the *whole* story. Sharon of course brings her own perspective and experience to this effort. You will recognize Sharon in this text…*she is in italics.*

An Ancient Path

A while back, Sharon and I were given the wonderfully rich opportunity to lead a tour group to the Holy Land—a prodigious experience for us all. At times, while we were there, I felt like Peter at the Transfiguration: *Lord, can we just pitch a tent and stay here!* A memorable trip—the excursion of a lifetime. Imagine standing in the ruins of the synagogue in Caesarea where on the Sabbath Jesus told the man with a crippled arm, "Stretch out your hand!" Think about being in the little town of Nazareth, at the very place the archangel Gabriel appeared to Mary. Consider walking the same shore of the Sea of Galilee where a resurrected Christ made a breakfast of fish and bread and lovingly reinstated Peter after his shameful denial on the night Jesus was betrayed. To visit these places is life-altering. One of the more moving, and yet exceptionally crowded experiences, was traveling along the Via Dolorosa, the Way of Suffering. This is the traditional route Jesus walked as he bled and in agony carried his heavy cross, for you and for me. It was that painful route to the horrid place of execution and also to his glory. This way was a spectacle of divine love. It was Jesus' path to his supreme suffering and to our great hope. When a pilgrim earnestly walks the Via Dolorosa, they soon diminish in their estimation of themselves. It puts one in a proper place—it is Christ, not I, who is exalted. With each station along that well-worn way, the pilgrim learns more about Jesus' labors on our behalf. At each of fourteen traditional stations, surrounded by believers from every nation, one moves more deeply into knowledge of Christ and more acutely into understanding his love for his Church. It's all more than one can digest, more than one can take in. To walk the fourteen stations of the Via Dolorosa, those ancient pavements once spattered with his blood, is to be changed forever. Finally, each of the stations progressively leads the pilgrim to the Church of the Holy Sepulchre, built over the very site where Jesus was crucified and where he borrowed a tomb for three days. As one follows the stations along that sacred path, one ends up at a most holy place, a place of worship built in AD 326 by the early Church under the direction of Helena, mother of Constantine. In the year 1009, the church was destroyed by the Fatmids, then rebuilt by the Crusaders in 1099. Throughout Christian history, this place of pilgrimage is where the nations have converged as one. My personal pilgrimage reminds me of that day when, with open heart and open mind, I followed this ancient path, walking by faith, surrounded by God's people from all over the earth, being thoroughly challenged and deeply moved by the mysteries of faith. As we prayerfully moved station to station that day in Jerusalem, following in his footsteps, we made our way along that ancient path to the doors of his Church. Little did I know as a minister that these steps, these stations, over the next decade would have expanded significance for me. I had no idea where they would lead me.

At this point, I am not even thinking about the Catholic Church. We had made great sacrifices for Durant's degrees from Protestant seminaries. I was a Protestant and proud of it. To me, being a Protestant was right up there with being from the South, attending Ole Miss, and being in the right social circles. In fact, I had been so busy doing everything that came with being a minister's wife and a mother of three small children that I hadn't really even had time to reflect on what I truly believed. I simply trusted the traditions of my denomination. I don't think I had ever really stopped to think about what Catholics actually believed. Little did I know about the journey that lay ahead of us!

1

no one
likes a bully

*I*ronically, what first drew my earnest attention to the Catholic Church was not my love of church history or ancient languages, or ecclesiology, or a study of the thorny theological issues of the Reformation. No, what first drew my attention to serious study of the Catholic Church was the bullying I witnessed as a Protestant minister. I was raised in a home where the rule of fundamental fairness was always (yet not without imperfection) at play and bullies were viewed as mean-spirited, uncharitable, even cowardly. This is something I have attempted to teach my children—there is no place in the Golden Rule for bullying. Once when I picked up one of my boys from summer camp when he was about twelve, I asked his cabin counselor, "Well, how was he during the camp? Was everything okay?" (With boys you just never know.) Replied the young counselor, "Yep, he was a very good boy. There was one issue, though…" I held my breath. "He put another boy in a headlock and made him confess he'd stop bullying his African-American friend. Yep, everything was just fine." I exhaled, smiling, knowing that another bully had been addressed. No one likes a bully.

Over the years, as I listened to the talk of non-Catholics, I often felt embarrassed by things being said about Catholics. It was as if Christian rules of civility and charity had somehow been waived in regard to this group. As a pastor committed to ecumenism, I took careful note. These occurrences were a sad curiosity. I was well aware of the theological issues that have divided Protestants and Catholics over the centuries. I had committed my adult life to seeking an understanding of them and had traveled to many of the historical locations where these fierce struggles took place. I understood the intense acrimony of the Reformation, I had read the centuries of mean ink spilled back and forth, and had visited many of the locations where the tragic blood-letting had taken place. I remember standing by the Seine with feelings of deep sorrow. It was there in Paris where the murderous St. Bartholomew's Day massacre took place. Hundreds of Protestant Huguenots were lured to Paris for a royal wedding, then ambushed and killed with no mercy. So many bodies were cast into the Seine that they formed grotesque "log jams" at the bridges. On the other side of the theological divide, I have also been to places where seasoned Catholic priests, such as the Irish Archbishop Oliver Plunkett, were hanged, drawn, and quartered, a most horrific and demeaning death, for faithfully following their calling in their own country. Plunkett, among many, many others, was killed at the Tyburn gallows in London, a place of such suffering that the mention of its name gave people the shudders. Visiting this place made me uneasy, even centuries later. I had stood in the Campo de Fiori, where Giordano Bruno was burned to death by Catholic authorities for the charges of heresy. I have also visited the very spot in Geneva where John Calvin eagerly produced letters of evidence to have Michael Servetus likewise burned as a heretic. [In his defense, Calvin actually urged the beheading of Servetus

The Campo de Fiori, where Giordano Bruno was burned in Rome.

rather than burning him. For this appeal for leniency he was chastised by his fellow Reformer William Farel.]

Yes, there has been terrific hostility, and if you know your history you are aware that everyone has some blood on their hands. In more recent history, during the Oxford Movement of the nineteenth century, many Anglican priests converted to Catholicism, and this was viewed by many Englishmen as papal aggression. As a sad result, Catholic priests were pelted with stones in the streets of England. In the United States, as Catholic immigrants steamed toward a dream called America, class wars erupted and social strife became hard reality. There has been some tough history in the Church—we, as Jesus had hoped in the High Priestly Prayer, have arguably not been united as one.

Intellectually, I comprehended all this, but it still did not provide a reasonable answer as to why some of our mature, committed parishioners could say such mean-spirited things about Catholics in the twentieth century. Often such statements weren't offered in overt anger. But just because they were often tongue-in-cheek, they were no less slurs, no less hurtful. As a minister of the Gospel, I have personally heard Catholics branded as "idolaters," "papists," "fish-eaters," "Mary worshippers," "superstitious," even "unbelievers." I lately heard a local pastor, while preaching, label Catholicism "nonsense" and "priestcraft."

The days are long gone for this type of language. It not only perpetuates discord, but gives the watching world yet more reasons to deride the bride of Christ. Recently, while writing this text, I was staggered by an individual's stating that he did not believe that Catholics would enter the kingdom of God. I felt confounded, genuinely saddened. Particularly in the South, often it's not exactly *what* is said, but it is the *way* it's said that is so telling. For example, I have heard the word *Catholic* whispered in conversations as if it were an offensive, dangerous, even scandalous word. My maternal grandmother used to whisper the word *cancer* in a similar fashion. As the people of God, we can do better than this. Jesus said that the world will recognize we are truly his only if we love one another.

Years ago, just out of seminary, I was a Presbyterian campus minister at the University of Mississippi. It was a wonderful time of teaching, Bible study, leadership training, and of course, enjoying SEC football. In the

South, SEC football is nearly as sacred as barbeque. Anyway, I had on staff a sharp, dedicated intern who worked with the ministry. Once on a ski trip, she was riding the ski lift up a slope with a stranger who asked her what kind of work she did. After she revealed that she was involved with a Christian ministry, the stranger on the chair lift went on an extended tirade and proceeded to lambast the Church. She was wise enough to graciously stop him and say, "Yes, the Church has its problems. And yes, the Church is made up of fallible people who make all kinds of mistakes. But you have to understand, the Church is the bride of Jesus Christ and he loves her very much. So we must be very, very careful what we say. Remember, we are talking about Jesus' wife." After this explanation, she told me, the rest of the ride up the mountain was pretty quiet.

We must be very careful, very thoughtful about how we speak about Jesus' wife. He loves her very much indeed.

a call for clarity

There were times when, as a young pastor, I would bite my tongue while in group settings or even at meetings with elderly church leaders, as someone would offer an uncharitable joke or erroneous remark about Catholics. Looking back on these moments now with a few more years under my belt, I confess: My silence was collaboration. I had read many of the works of Gandhi, King, and Mandela. I knew that oppression survives through silence. Yet, too often, I sat on my hands and at the end of the day I was unwilling to rock the boat.

Out of charity, out of love for Christ, I should have spoken up more often. This is as complicated as it is difficult living in the South. A Southerner understands. Traditionally, age is revered in the South and youth knows its place. I must say that hearing these things did give me an increased sensitivity about how I treated Catholics, and a concern to bring about understanding and change. The negative comments I heard regarding Catholics, were not expressed toward other groups, such as Methodists, Republicans, Hindus, vegans, Democrats, Lutherans, or communists. For some perplexing reason, these were reserved for Catholics, as if they were somehow fair game. For example, one pastor from my former denomination publically declared that thinking, self-aware Catholics were "enemies of the gospel." As a thinking Protestant, I found it difficult to associate myself with such sweeping claims. Statements like this are mind-boggling when you consider those many Catholics who, across the centuries, have willingly and courageously died for Christ. From the burning of Lawrence by Emperor Valerian, to the death of Edith Stein in a Nazi gas chamber, when one reads the theological profundity of scholars such as Duns Scotus or St. John of the Cross, when one surveys the fruitful ministries of St. Benedict of Nursia or St. John Baptist de

LaSalle, or when reading the works of Thomas à Kempis or Thomas Merton, one quickly recognizes that these efforts are momentous. To say these titans of Christendom are "enemies of the gospel" is outlandish.

More than a few times as a minister, I have seen listeners smile or chuckle privately at rude remarks. I distinctly recall being in an important meeting at the church, among mature believers who should have been far beyond this, hearing an off-color remark about Catholicism and thinking to myself: "No! This is not how God's children are to speak. Christ, the Great Shepherd, our Elder Brother, wants us to be one" (John 17:20-22). Yet I sat silently. At the time I was ashamed these older brothers could say such things. Looking back, though, I now feel ashamed of myself for not speaking up. Sometimes fearful silence—whether a fear of reprisal or even fear of embarrassment or impoliteness—can truly be the most insidious form of collaboration. It's accommodation through cowardice, and I was a chief among sinners.

From my experience, the way non-Catholics would dialogue with Catholics at times was unwittingly uncharitable. Usually, the hurt was not intentional, which points only to the issue's deep-seated nature. Even in our sophisticated, globally-minded generation of social media, texting, and e-books, there is still some old-fashioned work to be done on this issue. Not long ago, at a social gathering I was questioned by a former parishioner, "So you believe the apocryphal books? The ones the Catholics put in their Bible?" This person, though their timing was off a bit, was well-intended. Yet their language was less than considerate. They likely had no idea that the word *apocryphal* itself means "spurious" or "of questionable authenticity."

I responded, "Are you familiar with the Septuagint?"

"What is that?"

I then explained that it is a Greek translation of the Hebrew Bible which was produced around the third century BC, and contains the deuterocanonical books they are referencing. Being Greek-speaking, Jesus and the apostles were well aware of the Septuagint and quoted it often. I got a confused look when I explained that the Catholic Church had not "added" these "extra" books. Rather, it was the Protestant Church which, in effect, actually took them out. I smiled and shared with this individual, "The issue is not why are these books in *my* Bible, but why are they are not in *yours*."

I do admit that these textual issues are complex and the study a bit tedious, but it is definitely not as cut and dried as many non-Catholics believe it to be.

Another oft-repeated misunderstanding of Catholicism I encountered as a Presbyterian minister was that the Mass is a repeated sacrifice of Jesus Christ, as if Jesus were repeatedly sacrificed again and again at each Mass for the forgiveness of our sins. I distinctly recall one Presbyterian elder who held unusual disgust for this misunderstanding. He referenced it, like clockwork, whenever the subject of Catholicism was brought up. I remember as a pastor thinking (again engaging in Catholic apologetics for my Protestant parishioners) that this was indeed not the case. The Eucharist is a re-presentation of the drama of Jesus' atoning sacrifice. But to say that he is sacrificed again and again is incorrect.

Conversely, I have heard priests make it quite clear, quoting the book of Hebrews, that Jesus "entered the most holy place once for all by his own blood, having obtained eternal redemption" (Hebrews 9:12). If there is any sacrifice being made at the Eucharistic table it is being made by the believer, who by faith is presenting his or her body as "a living sacrifice" in response to the great love of Jesus.

In my study and experience, I have discovered that most Protestant rejection of Catholicism is not actually a rejection of actual, historical Catholicism, but a rejection of misconceived Catholicism. The late Archbishop Fulton Sheen once said, "There are not one hundred people in the United States that hate the Catholic Church, but there are millions who hate what they wrongly perceive the Catholic Church to be." In my twenty-five years as a pastor, I have found this to be dead accurate. Interestingly, most Catholics seem to understand this and are exceedingly patient with such misunderstandings. As a Protestant minister, for the sake of peace, I found myself again and again involved with Catholic apologetics to clarify the gross misunderstandings that many of our parishioners had about Catholicism. This is what initially led me into a deep study of the Catholic Church. I have often thought about the irony of this. I saw a good deal of rancor toward Catholics because people genuinely thought they worshipped Mary, or worshipped images or saints, that they are not allowed to study the Bible, or that Catholics believe they are justified by works, that they worship the dead, or believe the Pope is sinless, and so on. All these thoughts are absurd. I learned a good deal about the Catholic Church through explaining to Protestants what it is *not*. And the more I learned, the more I respected and appreciated Catholic tradition.

This is not the occasion for an exhaustive addressing of these misunderstandings. Yet it is the role of Christian clergy from every corner of Christendom to fight against the fear, ignorance, animosity, and divisions that so often go with misunderstanding. As brothers and sisters in Christ, we are to work toward mutual understanding, real peace, and a genuine filial love for one another. In his first epistle, Peter exhorts the Church always to discuss and present issues of faith with "gentleness and respect." For believers, this isn't optional. Pastors, ministers, elders, priests, clergy, deacons, church leaders, and laity should all work wholeheartedly to help congregations better appreciate the beauty, mystery, and diversity of the body of Christ. This is an often overlooked ministry which would greatly benefit the global church.

To learn more about what Catholics actually do believe, try a good and easy-to-read book by a former Protestant minister, Dr. Scott Hahn, entitled, *Signs of Life: 40 Catholic Customs and Their Biblical Roots*. The book is a solid overview covering a broad number of topics from the Mass to the rosary, from holy water to incense, from the Eucharist to confession. It is a wealth of information, a great resource for God's people.

I remember when Durant told me one of his friends who had a Master of Divinity degree had become a Catholic. Personally, I did not find this to be troubling. What I did find troubling was that his conversion to Catholicism had cost him his job at an evangelical organization. When he was asked to leave as a result of becoming a Catholic, I remember thinking something was very wrong with that. It didn't sit well with me…Christians rejecting other Christians.

I could understand this had he become an atheist, or an enemy of the Church. But how could people who proclaim to be Christians be so judgmental toward Catholics? Over the years as a Protestant minister's wife, I had heard things said about the Catholic Church that made me cringe. But, looking back, I had probably said some of these things myself, having had, I confess, no real knowledge of what the Catholic Church actually believed.

Sharon and I on the shore of the Sea of Galilee at the location where Christ re-instated Peter.

beware the hardening of the categories

*I*n those days, my only real knowledge of what the Catholic Church believed was just what I had heard over the years. Somehow, I had come to believe that they worshipped Mary, that they believed you go to Heaven by working really hard but had no real assurance, that they confessed their sins to a priest, and the Da Vinci Code had something to do with the Catholic Church and all its mystery!

Learning about the Catholic Church at first was no more than educational for me. I was a skeptic. To be honest, when I first thought about what it would be like to be Catholic, rather than joy, I thought about having to live in the face of all of the stereotypes and prejudices I had heard. The one thing I remember at this point was praying for God to make me open to whatever he had in store for me. I had to be completely honest with myself. But could I be that open? I wasn't sure exactly what Catholics believed. Would I have to wear a veil during church? Would I have to "curtsy" before I entered a pew? What in the world is holy water? Do we have to have more children? No way on that one! Durant felt more comfortable studying the Catholic Church than I did. He didn't say much about it, then—to him it seemed more or less academic. I was leery. I wasn't buying it. If the truth be known, I was still the proud Protestant!

I owe many thanks to my former denomination and to my esteemed mentors and professors. Through this denomination I was encouraged to foster a love for the Scriptures, a keen interest in theology, an understanding of the importance of solid teaching, and a passion for the history of Christ's Church. Ironically, and gratefully, it was this encouragement and scholastic push that led me to Catholicism.

It takes academic self-discipline to set aside one's own denominational biases, entrenched theological paradigms, and exegetical anticipations in order to study objectively. Often, the longer a person dwells in a theological tradition, the more that individual may experience what I have come to call the "hardening of the categories." As you spend time in a particular tradition, it becomes increasingly difficult to approach a text, a thought, or a doctrine from any other perspective. For someone whose mind has become clouded by denominational zeal, academic laziness, or the hardening of the categories, seeing issues from a divergent perspective can become almost impossible. Too often, with time, regrettably, we can see things only through our own perspectives, through our own theological lenses.

In God's providence, I was fortunate to attend two of the finest seminaries in the country—Trinity Evangelical Divinity School, just outside Chicago, and Covenant Theological Seminary, nestled in the quiet suburbs of St. Louis, Missouri. I received an outstanding education from both institutions. I did not have good professors. I had *exceptional* professors who strove to bring out the best in each of us. (One of my Old Testament professors at Trinity was so demanding that we who sat in the back of the room would at times plead for straw for the difficult "brick-making" of his class. Knowing this was a biblical reference to Pharaoh's cruelty during Israel's enslavement, he was not pleased, to say the least!).

The best, the preeminent professors would always encourage us to approach material with scholastic objectivity. When studying church history, we were warned to avoid the anachronistic tendency of importing or projecting our own ideas and perspectives back into distant moments or movements of history. Likewise, when exegeting (drawing meaning out of) a biblical text, that text must be allowed to speak for itself. Each passage is to be understood in light of its historical, grammatical context and examined in regard to the whole of the divine Scriptures. There is a rigor to this endeavor that takes a certain intellectual independence from one's own denominational tradition if one is to study with integrity. A passage of the Bible is not to be readily framed by one's own denominational presuppositions. The study of history is to be approached in the same manner. This is much, much easier said than done, yet it is the mark of true scholarship. This is the hard work of thinking.

As a brief aside, I am also deeply grateful that I was raised by a creatively relentless scientist. My father, the late Dr. Irvin D. Fleming, spent his life as a cancer research scientist and surgical oncologist. He taught his children to think critically, to risk being wrong, to be willing to own a dissenting view, to apply the empirical method when applicable, and to avoid superficial group-thought. I am forever thankful that my father, a pioneer in the field of research methods, passed on these characteristics of sound scholarship and thought. Not that I have mastered them by any means, but they have been priceless tools in my academic tool box.

As earlier stated, I was fiercely loyal to the Reformation and to the doctrine it produced. Yet I've found that denominational loyalty is a two-edged sword. I have seen this many times in others and now saw it glaringly within myself as I set sail for the odyssey of honestly exploring the Catholic Church. Commendable as denominational devotion might be, it may actually be the very thing that impedes objective learning and personal growth. The conundrum is this: The more tenaciously one grasps at one's own denominational position, the less likely one may be open to sincere theological exploration and change. Denominational zeal may actually be an obstacle more than a friend. Heart and mind have an extraordinary relationship when engaging things religious. The heart should be free to burn, yet the fuel with which it is stoked must be delivered by a mind that is liberated and free to learn.

Once, as a Presbyterian campus minister, I was speaking with a student who had a keen interest in the topic of the end of time—the field of study called eschatology. She let me know that she held *the* "biblical view" on the issue. While talking with this student, utterly certain of her position, I thought I would try something new. I wanted to see just how hardened her categories had become. As a Protestant minister I asked her whether she grasped that her eschatological perspective was actually the minority view—not only today but through the history of Christendom. No. She refused to believe that her view on the end times had ever been a mere minority view. "It can't be," she said. "It's in the Bible! It's what people should believe!" As we say in the South, I'd gotten her dander up. I kindly assured her that her particular take on the end of the ages was indeed, in light of all of church history, a minority position. No, she said—it was the "Bible truth." So there you have it.

This may be an extreme case. But if we'll be academically sincere for a moment, we all suffer in varying degrees from a hardening of categories. The real question is: Are we aware of this? Is there still room in our minds and hearts for honest intellectual and theological exploration and growth? Maybe, just maybe, God is not done with us yet.

authority
is good

I have spent my adult life studying the Bible in earnest. Not that I've mastered it, by any means. But I have approached it in a dedicated fashion. I have pulled out much of my once thick, wavy hair learning Greek and Hebrew so that I could read the biblical texts in the original languages. I have sought out and have enjoyed the privilege of studying under many outstanding scholars. The more I've studied theology, applying the rigors of scholarship, the more I have noticed that what I was reading and learning from church history and the Bible did not fit into some of the tightly prescribed categories of my Reformational heroes.

I had been taught, in some not-so-subtle ways, that the reformers rose up at a particular period of history and had deftly realigned the Church, rather in the manner of a skilled chiropractor. In varied ways it had been told to me that they had settled the matter. The more I looked at this, the more unsettled I became about the Reformation and its outcome.

We often forget there have been protectors and defenders of the faith, reformers of the church, from the time of the apostles to present day. Survey the millennia and you'll see that a legion of biblically-minded, passionate reformers within the Catholic Church have gone before, during, and after the fifteenth and sixteenth centuries. I discovered that often, the life efforts and writings of these protectors of the faith have gone both unappreciated and unnoticed by many. For example, very few outside the Catholic world recognize the Reformational work of Anthony Zaccaria, who, after studying to become a physician at the University of Padua, was ordained and entered the priesthood in 1528. After years of ministry in hospitals and serving the poor, Anthony founded three religious orders to work to bring about reformation in the Church. Anthony met stiff opposition, reformation often being difficult, but was exonerated with each accusation. I mention Anthony because he is one of hundreds of faithful protectors of the faith from across the centuries. Countless faithful men and women have given the best of their lives' efforts toward reformation. If you study church history you will find there are many more who were dedicated to the purity and unity of the Church, yet did so without breaking from the institutional church.

Concerted and effective efforts at reformation were taking place within the Church before, during, and after the years of Martin Luther. Take the writings of Dante Alighieri as an example. The life and efforts of St. Francis of Assisi are another. There were godly, righteous men and women such as Margaret Ward, David Lewis, Anne Line, John Fisher, Henry Morse, Margaret Clitherow, John Payne, and the venerable John Houghton, to name a few more. Such heroic Catholic defenders of the faith went to the gallows by the dozens for their efforts to strengthen and preserve the Church's unity. It is astounding what these individuals endured for the sake of the Church. Though the phrase *Ecclesia semper reformanda est* ("The Church is always to be reforming") became a slogan of the Protestant Reformation, it was nonetheless not a notion new to the Catholic Church. The Catholic Church has been about this reform for two millennia. When Justin Martyr wrote *Dialogue with Trypho,* when Origen penned *On First Principles* at the Second Council of Ephesus when Leo the Great issued his famous *Tome*, when Cyril of Alexandria defended the nature of Christ against Nestorianism, and when Augustine produced his magnificent *On The Holiness of the Catholic Church*, these were all efforts of church reform and renewal. Ongoing reform has been alive in the Church from its inception, yet it has been conducted in such a way—never perfectly—as to preserve and support Church unity. It was the goal of the protectors of the faith all across the history of the Catholic Church to work continually toward restoration and reform, and to do so *without* rupturing the Church. They truly believed it was Christ's desire, fallible and feeble as we are, that the Church be one. A family is to remain together.

It is a reductionist view of history to believe that the Protestant reformers fixed the church's problems and made it right. The reformation of the Church is far more complex than Luther's making a momentary clamorous correction during his lifetime and getting the ship back on course. For instance, the Five Solas of the Reformation are tidy tools for communicating the ideas of the Reformation. I have taught them hundreds of times, but their simplifications begin to crack under the weight of serious biblical and ecclesiastical study. Consider, for example, the attempt to defend Sola Scriptura (the idea that the Bible alone is the sole voice of authority) from the Scriptures alone. It was certainly a helpful idea framed by the reformers to advance the Reformation, but even the Scriptures teach that the Church is "the pillar and foundation of the truth" (1 Timothy 3:15). Many forget that the early Church predated the canon and yet they worshipped, carried on the Eucharist, preached, established churches, guided and defended the Church with no authorized canon. How did they do this without Sola Scriptura? Upon what did they rely during those early centuries before the New Testament was produced?

This was achieved by means of creeds, councils, bishops, and Church traditions handed down by the apostles and bishops, who received the deposit of faith from Jesus Christ himself. We must always remember that it was the Church which gave birth to the Scriptures, not the other way around. Nowhere does Scripture tout that it is the supreme authority over the Church.

This awareness requires a paradigmatic shift in thinking for a lifelong Protestant to grasp. Christ established his Church and the Eucharist long before one word was ever written down, centuries before the New Testament texts were compiled. The Church as established by the apostles was the authority, under the superintending work of the Holy Spirit. The Scriptures were given under the authority of the Church to guide, serve, and support the Church until the end of time.

At this point in my journey, I submerged myself in serious academic study. Actually, like this chapter, my study was rather bookish and solitary. It was a lonely period on my personal sojourn in a two-fold way. First, to discuss or even mention many of these issues to my Protestant colleagues was not exactly popular. In the theological waters in which

I swam, a whiff of anything "Romanish" would hardly advance one's career. Second, many people have no real interest in going down into the academic mines themselves and digging around in some of the nuances of ecclesiology, church history or theology. But as I dug, I continued to unearth curiosities that kept me digging.

For example, a number of historical ironies emerge when one examines Protestantism today. The first is that modern American Protestantism reflects very little of what the reformers actually embraced. The reformers' views on the significance of the Church, their language regarding conversion, and particularly the critical importance of the sacraments, might not even be recognized by modern Protestants. Luther's view of the Eucharist and his devotion to Mary, whom he called the Queen of Heaven, would be rejected by many in modern-day Protestantism. All one has to do is read the reformers' perspectives on baptism to understand this gulf.

In his *Institutes of the Christian Religion*, John Calvin wrote, "In baptism, God regenerating us engrafts us into the society of his church and makes us his own by adoption" (4.17.1). Today, most Protestants believe that baptismal regeneration is a Catholic doctrine. Also, the reformers did not use the language and theological categories of modern evangelical Protestantism. There has been such a shift in Protestantism away from its classical views that it's doubtful whether Martin Luther or John Calvin would be able to pass the ordination examinations in many Protestant denominations. Their views on baptism, the necessity of the Eucharist, and the critical role of the visible church for salvation would be viewed as far too Catholic. Actually much of the language and theology of American evangelical Protestantism can be traced to early American Puritanism and can be found in part in the revivalist works of Whitefield, Wesley, and Edwards. Much of what modern Protestants believe today is framed by the American revivalist movement, not the classical Protestantism which came out of the Reformation. Many Protestants readily point to Luther, Calvin, Farel, and Zwingli as their champions, but they do not hold to what these reformers actually espoused.

Another interesting irony that kept surfacing in my studies was that the Bible to which Protestants appeal for Sola Scriptura and which they so wholeheartedly embrace was actually a by-product of the ecclesiastical authority and living tradition of the early Catholic Church under the papal leadership of Pope Damasus (AD 366-384). It was the magisterium, the teaching authority of Catholicism, which selected the texts to be placed into the Bible. We can actually thank the Catholic Church for the Scriptures we now have. Some Protestant theologians who understand this historical reality do make a quasi-concession by confessing that, because the Bible was assembled by Catholic councils, the Bible is actually a "fallible collection of infallible books."

This view only undermines the canon itself. What if I don't like James, or Hebrews, or Galatians? Can I simply disregard it as part of the fallible canon? Luther viewed the book of James—"that right strawy epistle"—in this light. This perspective also raises another question: Are there other books which should have been placed in the canon that were not? Catholicism holds to the view that not only are the books of the Bible infallible, but God infallibly superintended the Church in their selection and compilation.

A further irony: Most Protestant churches claiming Sola Scriptura do in fact defer or appeal to some historical authority. That appeal to authority might be to the writings of Luther, the works of John Calvin, or the Westminster Confession of Faith. When I was going through my ordination process, it was quite clear that if I deviated too far from the positions within the Westminster Confession of Faith, even though I may claim Sola Scriptura on an issue, I would not be ordained. This was a real and sobering appeal to an authority. No one is more keenly aware than a seminarian, whose ordination and livelihood hang on his beliefs, of where these theological lines are drawn. Some churches look to the strong leadership of their pastor as the final authority in disputes or issues of doctrine.

I recently heard a sermon by a pastor of an independent Bible church who had come to the conclusion that his church had no need for the office of deacon. So, there you have it—no deacons in his church. Such authority might be found by others in the position papers of their denomination. In some circles, authority might be found in unique revelations or mystical insights given to the pastor. On any given Sunday that pastor might reveal a "new word" received from God. In other church circles, authority might be found in the scholar or pastor who is highly skilled in reading the Bible in the original Greek and Hebrew, establishing a kind of "academic priesthood."

Within today's denominations, elders possess authority, deacons hold authority, the regional assembly exerts authority, the books of church government carry significant authority, and the national assembly of that particular denomination wields an enormous amount of authority. These all represent a historical, authoritative, and living tradition for those who worship and serve in that particular denomination.

Do the investigation for yourself: Neither Jesus, nor the apostles, nor the early fathers ever claimed Scripture as the sole voice of authority for the Church. Sola Scriptura was an assertion made by the reformers but cannot be supported by the Scriptures themselves. A pastor may claim Sola Scriptura, and declare that, through his own personal study and private interpretation, he has been led by the Scriptures to a view that diverges from his denomination. Such a pastor might want to update his resumé. He may soon be unemployed if his view runs significantly against the grain of his elders' authority and the denomination's traditions. He may have just "sola scriptura-ed" himself out of his job. We all have our traditions regarding styles of worship, our views on the sacraments, understandings on church government, and these traditions frame our ecclesiology.

The real question is: Where did these traditions come from? One may tout Sola Scriptura, but at the end of the day, there is a large corpus of tradition that aids and directs denominations toward their interpretation and application of Scripture. Again, if a pastor swims too hard against the hermeneutic currents of his church's tradition, even though he may cite Sola Scriptura, he may be soon looking for another pastorate. I have seen this more than a few times. He could passionately argue, "Our church has a tradition that is not found in Scripture, and the Bible has led me to a more accurate conclusion." And he might just hear in reply an elder's or a deacon's appeal to their tradition: "That's just not how we do things here." I have heard many a pastor say, "We are a 'book only' church," then default to their own tradition and serve grape juice at communion when they know very well that the biblical texts indicate οἶνος, real wine. One of the criticisms laid at the doorstep of the Catholic Church is that tradition is viewed authoritatively alongside Scripture and as a guide for the Church. In reality, if the critics were transparent, they would confess that *all* denominations appeal to their living and historical tradition. The Catholic Church is just very forthright about this and celebrates the reality that God, through the Holy Spirit, providentially superintends his Church, having promised that "the gates of hell will not overcome it." We should be grateful for church authority and tradition. For example, most of our grasp of the Trinity was developed through the Catholic Church's councils and ecclesiastical tradition. Without church tradition and the authority of councils and bishops, the early Church might have been smothered in its cradle before a canon was ever established.

At the turn of the last century, Cardinal Gibbons, Archbishop of Baltimore, made a salient point when hundreds of women descended upon Washington, DC in protest. They, through their private interpretation of the Scriptures, had come to the conclusion that Abraham, Isaac, Jacob and other families of the Old Testament were correct, and that they, too, through a thorough study of the Bible, had come to understand that the Bible's teachings on the joys and benefits of polygamy were true. This was no small issue to many women from Utah in the late 1880s. A true proponent of Sola Scriptura (apart from a living Church tradition to guide and inform) really has little to say to these crusaders of polygamy other than: *That's your interpretation and I must respect it.*

To say anything else would be to foist your traditional views upon their understanding of Sola Scriptura. I was ordained in one of the twelve Presbyterian denominations in America, a subset of the almost fifty Presbyterian denominations worldwide. (These numbers are moving targets as denominations multiply.) The variances of biblical interpretations within Presbyterianism span from upholding the deity of Jesus Christ to the outright denial of it—all of these available within what is loosely called Presbyterianism. Apart from Presbyterianism, there are presently tens of thousands of denominations. With time, we can expect even a wider range of biblical interpretations and theological perspectives. Rather than a move toward a consensus or theological unity, many groups are moving away from it. What is the basis for ecclesiastical authority? Is there *any* authority?

There were already hundreds of Protestant groups by the end of the seventeenth century, each appealing to various sources of authority. This lit the fuse for an explosion of Christian sects, groups, denominations, and splinter movements that we see today.

During the nineteenth century in the United States there was an especially rapid multiplying of sects and unorthodox movements, fueled by the notion of private interpretation unhinged from a living, authoritative tradition. With no living tradition, no authority or definitive voice to draw these creative hermeneutic schemes back to center, many Protestant groups strayed into heterodoxy and into belief systems radically diverging from orthodox Christianity. Many such movements reflect the theological chaos found in "book-only" traditions. Without an authoritative tradition, Sola Scriptura can turn on itself and can be seen to have seeded the plurality of sects emerging during America's industrial revolution and the century that followed.

We must remember that the way we interpret the Bible has real consequences—practical implications for life. Some Christian sects refuse blood transfusions, reject the second person of the Trinity, reject medical treatment, refuse to purchase health insurance, will not install smoke detectors in their homes, reject all oaths and pledges, refuse to pay taxes, are fiercely protective of racial purity, and some do not educate their children beyond age fourteen. To voluntarily choose these options as a free person is anyone's prerogative, but to bind a human being's consciousness as if these stances were the authoritative, certifiable will of God is a different matter altogether. Such instances may seem extreme, but they do illustrate how a departure from ecclesiastical authority has real-life consequences.

When we study the leadership of Israel, we find that they viewed God's Word with extreme reverence, yet also looked to the high priest and the Sanhedrin as God's ordained organ on earth to lead the people and to offer guidance on critical matters. One could even be put to death in Old Testament days for disregarding the divinely granted authority of the leadership of Israel. The early Church was not an Old Testament theocracy that executed sinners. But Jesus' teaching did not annihilate the already accepted notion of divinely guided leadership, despite those leaders' human limitations. The superintending work of God was understood as a reality in the early Church. They were fully aware that God could draw a straight line with a crooked stick. The Church did not have a New Testament affirmed until the end of the fourth century. For guidance, they turned to apostolic leadership, the Church's defended traditions and teachings, the direction of the Councils, and the leadership of the early bishops. The Apostle Paul called the Church "the pillar and foundation of the truth." This is why he wrote to the church at Thessalonica, saying, "Therefore, brothers, stand firm and hold fast to the traditions that you were taught, either by an oral statement or by a letter of ours" (2 Thess. 2:15).

I will leave the detailed exploration up to the reader, but as one studies the early Church one sees clear references not only to Peter's authority, but also to the successors of Peter, and universal appeals to this authority across the centuries. In writing to the Corinthians, Clement I, who succeeded Peter as the fourth Bishop of Rome after Linus and Anacletus, refers authoritatively to "the word of God spoken through us" and "obedience unto the things written by us through the Holy Spirit." Early on, Rome was viewed as the seat of divinely established authority. In the mid-third century Cyprian refers to the authority of Fabian, Bishop of Rome, Fabian now being "in the place of Peter." Early disputes and challenges to the Church were deferred to the authority of the Bishop of Rome. The term *Pope* ("Papa") was used in the 200s more generally for bishops in various cities, yet became associated with the unique position and authority of the Bishop of Rome as the successor of Peter. In 304, Roman bishop Marcellinus was designated Pope, and by the sixth century that designation was reserved exclusively for the Bishop of Rome. This individual was viewed as successor to the Apostle Peter and the supreme head of Christ's earthly Church. It was the intention of the early Church to have one faith, one worship, and one ecclesiastical government until the end of time.

Rome was the seat of ecclesiastical authority and this was traced to Jesus' authority, represented by the keys of the Church, given to Peter and subsequently to each of his successors. Even today on the Papal seal one will notice the keys of ecclesiastical authority. This apostolic authority was the recognized authority of the Church fathers and has been for the global majority of Christendom to this present day. It was this study of the living, apostolic succession of Church authority which has safeguarded Christ's deposit of faith across the millennia, playing a significant role in the conversion of Anglican priest and eminent theologian John Henry Newman to Catholicism. Newman, author of *Loss and Gain*, *Apologia*, and *The Idea of a University*, at age forty-four, after years of dedicated study, concluded the Roman Catholic Church was in closest continuity with the Church as personally established by Jesus Christ.

In his classic nineteenth century work, *Faith of Our Fathers*, Cardinal James Gibbons offers a helpful analogy in light of the apostolic authority and supremacy of Rome. This simple illustration proved helpful to my understanding as an American. Gibbon suggests the Scriptures are akin to the Constitution of the United States and that the Bishop of Rome is analogous to the Chief Justice of the Supreme Court. The truth of Scripture is never to be altered or added to, yet there are occasions when it needs to be interpreted. The Pope has the benefit of the cardinals and the collective wisdom of the bishops from the entire world to assist him as he seeks proper interpretations of our church "constitution." As the Supreme Court's determinations are absolutely authoritative and critical to the unity and permanence of the nation, so also are the determinations of the See of Rome to the unity and permanence of the Church. There is no further appeal. Just as a good father prayerfully leads a family with love, sacrifice, wisdom, and charity, so goes the Church. This was precisely the intent of the early Church as it trusted God's guidance. During the fifth century, when the Arian debate challenged the divinity of Christ, this movement was authoritatively condemned by the Pope. Augustine acknowledged the supreme authority of the Bishop of Rome on this issue, saying, "The question is ended." This may run against the emotional grain of modern, independent, democratically-minded westerners, but the durability and permanence of the Catholic Church rests upon the absolute authority of the Bishop of Rome as the successor of Peter, the Keeper of the Keys.

I have heard it insinuated that, because of Catholicism's high view of Church tradition and authority, it is in fact anti-Scriptural. A bizarre thought! It was the Catholic Church which gathered, protected these texts, and affirmed the Canon at the Council of Carthage in 397. Often we forget that it was the Catholic Church that copied and safeguarded the Holy Scriptures for the next fifteen hundred years. It was the fourth century Pope Damasus who chose Jerome, a leading scholar, to translate the entire Bible to benefit all Christendom. In the eighth century, The Venerable Bede had the Bible copied into Saxon for the edification of the Church in that part of the world. By the end of the 1200s the entire Bible had been translated into French. Of course, there were some translations that came under scrutiny by the Church, as should be.

When the printing press came about, reformers were not the only ones cranking out Bibles by the thousands—far from it. The Catholic Church printed Bibles, translating them into the many languages of Europe. There is a persistent myth that the Catholic Church did not want Bibles to get into the hands of the laity, as if the Church had something to hide. History roundly contradicts this idea. The Catholic Church has championed the Scriptures for two thousand years. It is something for which all Christendom should be grateful. Throughout history, there

St. Peter holding the Keys in Rome.

were difficult times when bishops, priests, monks, and nuns protected the Scriptures from war, invaders, despots, fires, floods, and plagues to safeguard the treasure of God's Word. Monks, who were dedicated copyists, gave entire lives to laborious transmission of hand-copying the Bible across the centuries. When one of these monks died, he was readily replaced by another willing to take on such an honorable role for Christ's Church. During the Mass each Sunday, there is a poignant moment after the reading of the Gospel when the priest reverently bends down to kiss the sacred text. This simple but ancient act says it all.

One strength of the Protestant Church is its teaching and preaching. While attending college, I became involved in a ministry in the Reformed Protestant tradition. I got a major dose of Reformed doctrine and it wasn't long before I could argue with the best of them regarding matters of the Presbyterian faith. I thought I really had a lot of it figured out—in nice, neat categories. I could tell you all about the five points of Calvinism, election, Sola Scriptura, the order of salvation, and basic principles of hermeneutics. I had studied the Westminster Confession of Faith and had my theology tied down pretty tightly. After Durant and I seriously began studying the Catholic Church, my tidy theological categories started to unravel before my eyes. To be honest, I had thought the teachings of St. Augustine on grace were certainly Presbyterian. No, these teachings were Catholic. Also, my faith changed when I began to study the Catholic Church's teaching on communion. I recall the point when I could not deny the evidence that when Jesus said, "this is my body, broken for you," he meant it. Looking back, I sadly thought of all the times that I had walked into the church on Sunday and, seeing we were having a quarterly communion, thought to myself, "Ugh, it means the service is really going to be a long one." How could I have missed that! As we continued to grow in our understanding, Durant and I would talk about how we were so eager to take the Eucharist. At this point on our journey, I can honestly say that I stepped back with a bit of trepidation because so much of the doctrine and tradition I had held so dear most of my life was crumbling before my eyes. I had to be honest and look at history, tradition and scripture and see it for what it really was, not how my past church tradition wanted me to see it. The veil was being pulled back for me, and it was both scary and exciting.

babies
and bathwater

Iremember standing before the Reformation Wall in John Calvin's Geneva, as a Presbyterian minister, thinking to myself a danger- ous thought: *I hope these guys got it right.* They had seceded from the apostolic authority of the Church, had espoused divergent views on the Eucharist, reframed the meaning of baptism, and eliminated certain ancient traditions in the face of fifteen centuries of church history. Any way you slice it, these are serious issues. I knew this as a student of church history and as a minister, and it made me nervous even as a Protestant. They definitely shimmied way out on a historically precarious limb, and I had shimmied out there with them. As a committed proponent of their efforts, the more I earnestly studied their works, the more I saw that the theological polarization and intense historical friction of their day had colored their positions, truncating some issues, or prompting them to jettison altogether some foundational teachings of the faith. Again, these are *serious* matters. In seminary, one circumspect professor warned us often to be wary of theological oversimplification and denominationally driven categories. To press the point, he confessed, "We Protestants often like our theology like our firewood—dried, stacked, and in order, and it doesn't often work that way." He was right.

Neatly defined categories might be easily understood, memorized, more readily transmitted, and they do provide a tidy litmus test for Protestant orthodoxy. Curiously, the more deeply I delved into the reformers' work and theological categories, the more I found they often didn't square with the Bible, and often did not reflect the beauty, mystery, genius, and organic design of our Maker. Most concerningly, they were not found in the early Church that Jesus Christ had established with his apostles. As a Protestant minister, this was unsettling to say the least, so for the first few years of my exploration and study I just kept all of this to myself. My journey was purely a solo one — often, though, I quietly wondered whether anyone else had ever noticed these things. Certainly someone had.

I was ordained in a white room. To be more specific, it was a sanctuary within the tradition of the Reformation. This was a highly significant day, marking the culmination of years of study, preparation and examination. Friends and family traveled to attend. At the reception, I was approached by one of my guests from another tradition, who cautiously asked, "Man, what was with the sanctuary? Why was it that way?"

Because of the denomination's theological orientation, the sanctuary had no ornamentation—no color, no art, no images, no stained glass, no images of Mary, Jesus or the apostles. Not even the most fundamental symbol of the Christian faith could be found in the sanctuary—the cross. To a visitor outside this tradition it looked like an old church with a bare, white worship space that really needed some sprucing up. But in reality it was a crystal clear, well-honed theological statement, a five-hundred year-old result of Reformational over-steering. In the attempt to expunge the Church of all things "Romanish," not only was the baby disposed of with the bathwater, but the bathtub itself.

We humans know intuitively that we are creative by divine design. We

The church where I was ordained.

42

are made to engage beauty, color, shape, form, and idea. We are aesthetic, three-dimensional creatures who are nourished and encouraged by art in real space. Art creates wonder and engages the imagination. Art speaks to the soul as well as to rational thought. This is why many pilgrims are moved to tears while standing amid the striking enormity and beauty of the basilica of St. Paul's Outside the Walls in Rome. I saw a visitor at the basilica of St. Mary Major, spontaneously dropped to his knees by the power of that holy space. I understood this, made my way over and knelt to join this brother from another part of the world. Within the Catholic tradition, art is a great source of spiritual encouragement, provoking sacred wonder.

Catholics do not, contrary to the presumption of many, worship art, images, statues, medals, icons, or rosaries. These things are wonderfully encouraging items that beautifully point us to God, encouraging us in our faith daily, but God alone is to be worshipped. I bring up the issue of the stark white sanctuary of my ordination because it symbolizes a larger matter. The reductionist tendencies of the Reformation went beyond the visual arts in attempting to rid the church of all things Catholic.

Study the Reformation closely enough, and you'll surely recognize similar truncating efforts in the realm of doctrine. One example: the debate over whether one's justification is a result of an infused righteousness (working in cooperation with divine grace), or an imputed righteousness (grace solely as a divine gift). This might seem theological hair-splitting to some, but do know that in some Protestant circles one's grasp of these categories may just determine whether one inherits eternal life or not. Some Protestants would argue that this issue (imputed versus infused righteousness) is actually the eye of the Reformational hurricane. Catholic theology and Catholic thought would declare that this issue is not as cut and dried as the reformers made it out to be, and that these categories rose from Reformational efforts to reduce issues of faith to reframed categories. Catholics would argue that it is all by God's grace, no matter how you frame the discussion. If you press a theologically informed Catholic and ask whether he believes himself justified by imputed or infused righteousness—I have done this several times—he'll listen patiently but will explain that you are posing the question in categories the Catholic Church doesn't use and hasn't since the apostles. I have found that part of the chasm separating Catholicism and Protestantism is that each group uses different word systems. I sincerely believe that, if we can prayerfully commit to continue working hard to bridge some of these linguistic issues, a great deal of theological harmony and historical reconciliation can be established. I believe there is much work to be done in this arena. The rewards will be well worth the effort. The obvious irony, when pressing the Protestant view regarding Reformational categories, is that there is an appeal to tradition and to the authority of the reformers for validation.

Another example of artificially forcing categories forged in the furnace of the Reformation is the understanding of the Ordo Salutis (Latin: *Order of Salvation*). In principle, the idea is beautiful, as it is an attempt to trace the grace of God in the life of the believer. It is a human and practical attempt to explain the process of God's general way of rescuing his people. I knew as a Protestant that this term *Ordo Salutis* was not found in the Scriptures and that in reality it was part of the authoritative tradition of the reformers.

Our salvation by grace is a profound mystery, infinitely complex, involving great arcs of time, difficult events, times of struggle, genuine doubt, hidden issues of the heart, and the miraculous work of the Holy Spirit, most often, mysterious and counterintuitive to our human ways. On paper the sequence or process of redemption represented in the Ordo Salutis appears orderly and cogent, yet the actual process of one's conversion is much more difficult to trace in light of one's actual divine-human encounter. Catholics grasp this mystery.

Conversion is an organic, mysterious, and continuing process, rather than a series of steps that can be clearly delineated. Interestingly, if one takes a close, historical look at the Protestant view of the Ordo Salutis, the whole complex from God's calling of a sinner to his regeneration, faith, repentance, justification, sanctification, and glorification, the entire process is our salvation. Catholics would use the word *conversion*. As a Protestant, I had to admit that salvation or conversion as defined by the Ordo Salutis was indeed a *process*—an exceedingly mysterious and involved process that may take place over a long time with no observable or perceptible lines of demarcation. This is where Protestantism and

Catholicism are actually far more closely aligned with one another than most people know or admit. Among theological traditions, particularly when there is a degree of adversarial pressure, we often make distinctions without a difference. Do we really believe that, when we stand before the throne of God at life's end, our man-made categories and nuanced theological terminologies will be a paramount issue?

I believe that tightly prescribed categories will be the last things on our minds on that great day. Yet these are the things that often keep us as believers from being one while here on earth. No, on that matchless day of reckoning, with nowhere to hide, not even a fig leaf to cover ourselves, we will be asked: *Did you love me?...Did you love your neighbor?...Did you keep my commands?...Did you have mercy on those in need?...Did you love and build up my bride, my Church?*

We may at times differ, even quibble over the precision of our language in regard to the process of conversion, but we do share the joy of the good news. Salvation is an unmerited gift from a loving God to all who believe and serve Jesus Christ. All who call on the name of the Lord will be saved—for this we can all celebrate forever.

I was not passive in this digging for more understanding. For ten rewarding years, I delved into historical views on baptism, the nature of conversion, the meaning of the Eucharist, the communion of saints, ecclesiastical authority, and Christ's unambiguous call for the unity of his Church. This was a time of exploration, prayer, writing, reflection, and theological tension. As with Jacob by the Jabbok River, there was even some wrestling involved. I came more fully to appreciate the story of Dr. Scott Hahn—a former Protestant minister who now is an esteemed professor of Catholic theology. Like Scott, my studies led me continually toward the Catholic Church, rather than away from it. I was not studying with some kind of conscious bias, or with a hope that my efforts would lead me to the Catholic Church. Actually, if this were to be the outcome, it would be career-ending for me as a Protestant minister. A daunting thought.

Becoming a Catholic was not high on my agenda as a Presbyterian minister, having served decades in my denomination. Also, in the back of my mind loomed another consideration. It did not involve the ancient writings of the early Church, or the issues surrounding the fierce theological jousting of the sixteenth century. No, it was much closer to home. Having counseled hundreds of couples, I knew it could put a significant strain on a marriage if one spouse embraced Catholicism and the other didn't. Not an insurmountable issue, but definitely not ideal.

I prayed God would have mercy and lead me wherever he wanted me to go. He has always been faithful and I knew he would be just as faithful as I walked into the unknown. As I struggled to fit all these issues into the algebra of my thinking, he gave me peace. It would have been much easier to put away my books, stop asking the difficult questions, safeguard my relationships, protect my ordination, and forget this issue altogether. It was the Holy Spirit and a desire to know the truth which coaxed me to venture onward in this journey.

I had not read any works by Scott Hahn until after I had embraced Catholicism. When I did, I had to laugh, thinking: *It happened to him, too!* A rigorous exploration of church history, theology, and Scripture had led him to the same place, the Catholic Church. Now I understand that reading a few of his books may actually have spared me years of study and struggle, but obviously that was not God's plan.

The more deeply I dug, the more I discovered my findings weren't fitting into my Protestant, evangelical categories. I intuitively knew in my heart and mind that there had to be much more behind these mysteries of faith. I would read about Eucharistic amazement in the Catholic Church across the centuries and, honestly, it was not part of my experience. I wondered why. Again and again, I came to understand that the fierce theological pushing and pulling of the Reformation and Counter-Reformation made it very difficult to study some of these issues with clarity. Much mean ink had been spilled on both sides of the tragic rift. Over the centuries everyone had anathematized everyone. A person must be committed to wade through this. To truly investigate Catholicism as a Protestant one must navigate through generations of straw men and study the scriptures objectively despite the shrill voices of theological condemnations and counter-condemnations. This calls for resisting the temptation to interpret ideas through the familiar. One must also risk asking hard, unpopular questions. It's much easier *not* to do this.

When one steps outside the circles of Reformed theology into the realms of broader evangelicalism, the categories become even murkier, more ill-defined. Broad evangelicalism has become so broad that many evangelicals are uncertain what they actually believe. Recent movements within the emergent church have pushed the boundaries of Christianity so far that some theologians suggest these groups might not even represent Christianity. In America now we find a form of evangelical nominalism that is all but unaware of classical Protestantism and the historical issues of its genesis. In my own years of ministry I found that much of broad, modern evangelicalism is characterized by layers of sentimentalism, the western business model, American individualism, and often the cult of pastoral personality. I am not sure the Church fathers would even recognize some of today's user-friendly, seeker-sensitive mega-churches. Having developed and taught an evangelical new members' class for many years within a mega-church fed by many evangelical traditions, I was often perplexed by how many Christians held vague or unorthodox views on fundamental issues regarding the nature of the Trinity, the meaning of the cross, the message of the Gospel, the meaning of communion, the role of the Church, the nature of worship, or the responsibilities of the Christian in society. These were not deeply nuanced or esoteric theological notions we were discussing—they were the most basic issues of the Christian faith. Why bring this up? Because I've found that this significant lack of understanding in classical Protestantism has even widened the already sad chasm of misunderstandings regarding Catholicism. Many evangelicals do not understand classical Protestantism, much less the history of the Church that preceded the Reformation.

At this point in my journey, I asked myself, *Where do I go from here?* I turned to the early Church.

go ask
your father

I cannot tell you how many times I heard my mother say this: "Go ask your father." In our home, he was the final authority. If you needed help, guidance, assistance, insight ...ask Father. So in the family of faith, I turned to the fathers for help. In turning to the early Church fathers for insight, I have to confess I had read hundreds and hundreds of pages of them (as assigned) in seminary and I had quoted them in hundreds of sermons. But for all that I had not studied the Fathers deeply. I hadn't examined them critically as an essential source to build my understanding of the Church. They had not significantly informed my ecclesiology.

This was a fundamental error on my part. Their historical proximity to Jesus Christ is not to be taken lightly. I had relied on the Church fathers for quotes and sermon material, but I had not sincerely looked to them as an aid to truly understand the scriptures and the theology of the early Church. In building my understanding of the Church, I had leaned more upon the Protestant reformers than I had upon those closest to Christ and the apostles.

What I learned not only confirmed many of my scriptural hunches, but also established in my mind that the Reformation had indeed truncated my faith in a number of significant ways. Reading the Church fathers was enriching, yet also exceedingly challenging to my trained Presbyterian categories. It was like listening to music performed on a different scale, after a lifetime of playing music. I remember while visiting Israel, as an open-minded lover of travel, cringing to some of the notes of the much-loved local music. To the resident Near-Easterners it was gloriously beautiful, but at first it was harsh to my Western musical sensibilities. It hurt my ears. With time, study, and an ever-improving understanding of the cultural context, I learned to love this music that was born from a different scale. Again, as one studies the Catholic Church, one has to be careful not to approach it through pre-formed denominational sensibilities. One must have an open heart, an open mind. My studies confirmed my emerging suspicions that there was more to the Christian faith than the reformers had announced. If you read the fathers with a teachable spirit, and with academic objectivity, be prepared to see your ecclesiastical world challenged. The more you study, though, the more you just might enjoy the music.

Approaching church history is no light matter. It is the story of our family, and Christian sects that stray too far from this family story often find themselves in trouble. As noted before, I've been privileged to visit many places significant in church history—an immense honor, and humbling. I have climbed upon the rubble of Jerusalem's temple, destroyed by Emperor Titus. I have visited the cave near the Dead Sea where David hid from a murderous Saul. I have walked the streets of Jesus' boyhood town, Nazareth, as well as the peaceful shores of Galilee. I have stood at the site of the Circus Maximus in Rome, where Christians were crucified for public display, and I have walked in awe down the Appian Way past the tombs of early martyrs.

One of the more stirring travel moments was when Sharon and I visited the tiny chapel rebuilt by the hands of the Church reformer St. Francis, in the basilica of St. Mary of the Angels just outside Assisi. This humble chapel was the epicenter of the world-changing Franciscan movement. I have listened to sermons delivered in places where John Calvin, John Knox, and George Whitfield have preached. I have celebrated Mass at the tomb of Leo the Great, been drawn into awe by the sacred works of Michelangelo, and prayed at the Coliseum where Ignatius of Antioch was killed by wild animals. I have stood at the Tyburn gallows in London, where Margaret Ward was brutally hanged. Visiting the Netherlands, I became acquainted with many little-known modern martyrs who resisted Hitler, such as Titus Brandsma, who was executed by lethal injection. I have stood solemnly at the sites of martyrs who had been strangled, hanged, drowned, burned, or disemboweled for their confession of Jesus Christ. At each place, I prayed for our Church and personally considered the difficult and complex issues of their day. I was thrilled to confess the Apostle's Creed at Caesarea Philippi, the place where Jesus looked at his disciples squarely and pressed them: *Who do you say that I am?* This was the very place where Jesus announced to Peter, "Upon this rock I will build my church, and the gates of hell will not overcome it" (Matt. 16:18).

A sober, thorough study of church history humbles, informs, challenges, emboldens, and significantly enriches our faith. It was Cicero who wrote, "Not to know that which came before you is to forever be a child." So I hungrily went to the Church fathers to learn and to grow.

The more I read works from the ancient Church, the more I came across the same language regarding ecclesiastical authority, the "deposit of faith" given the apostles by Christ, and the same deference to the See of Rome. In his well-known work *Against Heresies*, early Church father Irenaeus, a disciple of Polycarp (who was a disciple of John), wrote, "We point to the tradition of that very great and very ancient and universally known Church, which was founded and established at Rome, by the two most glorious Apostles, Peter and Paul." The early Church is replete with this language—it is inescapable.

As a non-Catholic, I had quoted St. Thomas Aquinas numerous times while teaching, and have heard many other non-Catholic ministers readily quote him. He stands as a theological titan in Christendom and one of the great doctors of the Church. Usually, St. Aquinas was cited on issues of faith and reason, the nature of God, or, more popularly, his arguments for the existence of God. I had taught Aquinas's "Five Ways" many times in Protestant settings. His theological work is broadly accepted as some of the most elucidating and profound thinking within the Church. No one ever approached me after presenting work by Aquinas in a non-Catholic setting and said, "That is just bad theology...why are you quoting him? Aquinas doesn't know what he's talking about." That is because, as one of our more penetrating scholars, Aquinas does indeed know what he's talking about. And if one continues to read Aquinas beyond his more popular work on faith and reason, or his arguments for the existence of

God, one will discover that Aquinas also wrote with great accuracy and confidence about the Catholic Church's positions with equal clarity and biblical insight. Aquinas was deeply certain about the real presence of Christ in the Eucharist. Once after Thomas wrote on the topic of the Eucharist and the real presence of Christ, he went before a church's altar and placed his document before the crucifix and prayed in earnest. Three priests heard a voice emanating from the crucifix, saying, "Thou hast written well of me, Thomas. What reward wilt thou have?"

Thomas replied, "None other than Thyself, Lord."

Yes, Thomas Aquinas has a great deal to teach us about faith and reason, the nature of God, and arguments for the existence of God, and this colossal figure also has much to teach us about the Catholic Church as well.

I found this to be true also regarding another giant in church history, St. Augustine of Hippo. In some Protestant circles, because of Augustine's deep understanding of grace and his view of predestination, he has been lauded and freely taught as if he were some kind of proto-reformer or an early herald of John Calvin. I have attended reformed theological conferences where Augustine was referenced so authoritatively and so often you'd have thought that he was indeed himself a Protestant. As a Protestant I had often heard that Augustine taught that salvation was a divine gift by grace, but what was omitted in these same discussions was that he was also a thoroughgoing Catholic. St. Augustine affirmed baptismal regeneration, purgatory, embraced apostolic succession as authoritative, celebrated the intercession of the saints, was devoted to Mary, acknowledged the necessity of the sacraments for salvation, and was convinced that the elements of the Eucharist were indeed the body and blood of Christ. St. Augustine proved an important figure on my journey.

Author, apologist, and Boston College professor of philosophy Peter Kreeft, a convert to Catholicism, confessed that the real presence of Christ was a monumental factor as he examined the Catholic Church. In his studies, he learned that, throughout the history of Christianity, from the apostles to the present age, all Christendom has embraced the real presence of Christ in the Eucharist, except for a minority movement of Protestants within only the past several centuries. This was disconcerting to Kreeft, who at the time was a Protestant. In sharing his thoughts on this in a lecture (its video cited in the *Helpful Sources* section of this text), Kreeft said, "If the Catholics are right, then we Protestants are missing out on the most amazing and astounding and intimate union with God that is possible in this life." The majority of Christendom has indeed celebrated the real presence of Christ in the Eucharist. For Catholics, from the time of the Apostles, this is one of the most glorious, mysterious, and soul-nourishing realities of the faith this side of heaven. The Eucharist stands as an unfathomable source of grace, transformation, unity, hope, and amazement. As a student of church history and theology, I knew this was a central issue to Catholicism, an issue I was going to have to address. It could not be swept under the carpet—it was undeniably embraced by classical Christianity.

Last Supper, *painting by Pascal Dagnan-Bouveret, 1896.*

words matter

s I studied the works of Clement of Rome, Clement of Alexandria, Ignatius of Antioch, Justin Martyr, the Didache, Irenaeus, Athanasius of Alexandria, Origen, Jerome, Ambrose, Gregory of Nazianzus, Cyprian of Carthage, Augustine, I was astounded. Not only was I moved by the depth of their devotion to Jesus and his Church, but I was thoroughly challenged by their views on the meaning of baptism, their emphasis upon the communion of saints (in heaven and on earth), the significance of Mary in redemptive history, their reflections on purgatory, the critical importance of apostolic authority and Church tradition, and the profound mystery of the real presence of Christ in the Eucharist. Universally, they adhered to the understanding that the elements at the Eucharist were miraculously transformed by the power of the Holy Spirit into the actual body and blood of Jesus Christ.

These realities of the faith are plainly found in the teachings of the Church fathers. For these beliefs many would willingly sacrifice their lives. As I read Augustine of Hippo on the eucharist, I thought of the famous words from his garden experience, *Tolle, lege* ("Take up and read"), which changed his life during his personal quest for truth. Here I was now, fifteen centuries later, taking up and reading Augustine's works, searching for truth as well. I could not neglect the irony of this. What I did not find in the words of the Church fathers was the teaching of the reformers, and the more I read, the more I found this to be the case.

The early Church used the term *Catholic* as the visible, unified body which was in communion with Jesus Christ. They had no concept of the distinctions that would later be applied to this word as a result of the Protestant Reformation. The thought that this word *Catholic* has been re-stamped is a deep challenge to modern evangelicals—a challenge that should be addressed. There is no shortage of information regarding the early use of the word *Catholic*. When Ignatius, Tertullian, Cyprian of Carthage, Cyril of Jerusalem, or Augustine used the word *Catholic*, they understood in the face of heresy, division, sects, and heterodoxy that they were referencing the historical Church descending from the apostolic authority of Peter. They were not referring to all who claimed Christian-like beliefs, of all sorts, with all kinds of diverging theologies and doctrines everywhere—the sense used by many modern denominations.

The early fathers did not intend the word *Catholic* to be broadly applied as "universal," as used by many churches today. As a Protestant minister dedicated to handling history as accurately as possible, I knew down deep as we recited the Apostle's Creed each week that we were bending, if not outright violating, the meaning of the word *Catholic*. To use the language of biblical interpretation (hermeneutics) we were *eisegeting*, importing modern notions back onto a more ancient concept. Exegesis is drawing out meaning from a text. Eisegesis is importing meaning back into a text. Any pastor worth his seminary diploma knows these basic principles. For example, to say that Nero played the fiddle while Rome was burning is a gross violation of history, and is importing the concept of an instrument that did not then exist back into that context. This is a simple illustration of *eisegeting* an idea or concept back into a place in history where it does not belong. At one point while leading worship services in a Presbyterian church, I almost had to cross my fingers behind my back as we said the Apostles' Creed, claiming to be part of the holy Catholic Church. Our concept of what we were saying during this service was not remotely congruous with what the framers of this creed intended.

As already observed, if one reads the early Church fathers, one quickly understands that they were passionate about and thoroughly committed to the Catholicity, the unity, of the body of Christ. Some denominations substitute the word *Christian* in the Apostles' Creed rather than attempt to reframe the word *Catholic*, knowing there is much more to this word than the simple translation "universal." There are a thousand church-goers who will readily accept the pat answer that in the Nicene Creed and the Apostles' Creed the word *catholic* means merely "universal." *Katholikos*, from *Kathluo*, meant "throughout the whole" or "universal" as used by Greeks in a non-ecclesiastical sense. Yet in Ignatius' letter, written about the year 110 to the Smyrnaeans, we see the word specifically and ecclesiastically applied: "Wheresoever the bishop shall appear, there let the people be, even as where Jesus may be, there is the catholic (*Katholike*) church." What is important is not, *What do we want this word to mean today?* but *What did this word mean when it was used by the early Church?*

Another example, among a host of illustrations of the early use of this word, is by Cyprian of Carthage, who in 253 wrote (*Letters* 66, 67:8), "For the Church, which is one and catholic, is not split or divided, but is indeed united and joined by the cement of priests who adhere to one another."

As I learned from the ancient fathers, I felt challenged and humbled. I had been taught that the truths of the Reformation were grounded in the early Church and as the medieval Church took a wrong turn, it was the reformers who brought Christian theology and doctrine back in line with the intent and teachings of the apostles and the early Church. As I studied the early Church in depth, I did not find this to be the case. I could not find the language or doctrinal teachings of Protestantism in the Early Church. Actually I discovered quite the opposite. Our Christian heritage, considered overall, is remarkably and thoroughly Catholic.

To discover teaching that stands in congruity with Jesus, the apostles, and the early fathers, look to the Catholic Church. I was brought to tears more than a few times as the historical evidence forced me to confront present versions of my faith. Though it was counterintuitive to my Protestant psyche, my research was leading me step after small step toward Rome.

To follow truth is an odyssey. I was not relishing the idea that my research was undermining my own theological framework. Nor was I eagerly looking forward to some of the social implications of embracing

Catholicism—I had heard plenty of the unkind comments. Nor was I enthused about jeopardizing my ordination and career. Yet over time I began to realize it was I who in fact held the minority position on many classic issues. I had discovered that many ancient theological positions and sound ecclesiastical traditions had not survived the troubled furnace of the Reformation, and certainly had not seen the light of day in broader modern American evangelicalism.

I distinctly remember one afternoon, after reading a passage from St. Augustine, sitting back in my study's squeaky chair and thinking: *They are Catholic…The Church fathers were Catholic…shortly after the death of the Apostle John, Ignatius used the expression 'Catholic Church'…St. Polycarp was called a "Bishop of the Catholic Church"…the genesis and historical arch of the Church is Catholic…the vast majority of the global Church has been and is today Catholic…I am the one who holds the divergent view, the one who has deviated from the teaching of the apostles and fathers, and I am the one who just might be out of accord with the center of gravity of the entire history of the Christian faith.*

A dear friend once confided in me. At first he joked, "Ecclesiastically, you're an amphibian. You've now been both a dedicated Protestant minister and a devout Catholic." Then his tone grew somber. "Can I ask you an honest question?"

"Absolutely. I may not have an answer, but go right ahead."

He paused, staring at his hands. "Obviously you've done your research, you've risked a lot and walked away from your ordination over this, so please bear with me…If the Catholic Church is the one, true Church established by Christ and the apostles, what does that make us Protestants?"

I hadn't heard the question put quite this way before. But I had *experienced* it—intimately. He deserved an honest, thoughtful reply. "If you had a son and he did not see eye to eye with you, and he became very frustrated and left your home, and he moved far away and really did not want a relationship with you, would he still be your son, would he still be family, would you still love him?"

I looked at my good friend. He nodded as his eyes filled with tears. He is my brother and will always be.

one tough family

*D*uring my time studying the Church fathers, I was invited to teach at Christian Brothers High School, an historic Catholic college preparatory school in Memphis, Tennessee. I was asked to write the curriculum and teach the non-Catholic students in the areas of Old Testament, New Testament, church history, and a Christian worldview course for seniors. Quite charitable of the Brothers, I thought, to offer these courses for their non-Catholic students—I cannot say that I have ever heard of a Protestant school's making a similar accommodation.

Not only was I searching the Scriptures during this time, and studying the catholicity of the early Church, but now I had a ring-side seat to study Catholics themselves. Little did my colleagues, fellow teachers, and Brothers know how closely I was examining the Catholic faith. Day after day, month after month, year after year, I listened to their words, watched their actions and reactions, and viewed their faith up close. I was not judging. Nor was I overly preoccupied with the process. But I was seeking to know more about Catholicism and how it works itself out in the real world. Theologians have a saying: *Orthodoxy precedes orthopraxy.* (Right thinking generally lends itself to right living.) If you really want to understand a person's theology, watch their life—it is their private, living, inescapable creed. Jesus put it thus: "You will know a tree by its fruit."

After almost twenty years of pastoral ministry in the Protestant Church, I was taken aback by what I experienced within this Catholic community.

And it wasn't just the CBHS community—it encompassed all the many parishes intersecting with this faith community. There was a genuine depth of spirituality and love for Jesus Christ, a practical loyalty among believers that challenged anything I had previously seen, and a sense of family that was a real, organic expression of their Catholic identity. As a Protestant, I was treated with remarkable dignity, kindness, and graciousness. I did not hear slurs, as I had in many non-Catholic settings.

As years went by and I worked within this community, I did a great deal of listening and learning. I was allowed to participate fully in the life of the school. The only point of difference was that I was asked to refrain from the Eucharist. After gracious conversations with the Brothers, I understood why. At that time I did not believe in the real presence of Christ in the Eucharist, as they certainly did. By allowing me to partake in communion, not believing that the elements were truly the body and blood of Christ, they would actually be encouraging me to take communion in an unworthy manner—something Paul warns us about sternly. They were being caring and consistent in not encouraging someone to eat or drink judgment upon himself, from their theological perspective. It was a deep matter of conscience to them. As a pastor I understood. I thanked them for their graciousness, commending them for being consistent to their convictions.

While at Christian Brothers High School, I saw faith in action. This distinctively Catholic faith was not "stuck in their heads," nor was it divorced from the temporal. If I needed something—a tire changed, a place to stay during marital strife, a bowl of chili for a sick family member, a ride to work, a person to earnestly pray, an ear to bend, or the shirt off of someone's back—they were there at every turn. This was not just because they were nice, Southern people. It was a fundamental, organic expression of their Catholicism. Over the years, I saw this again and again and again. The Catholic community I experienced there was seriously dedicated to the embodiment and incarnational nature of following Christ. If you love Jesus you *do* something about it—it isn't all that complicated.

There was also a focus on living continuously in the presence of God—an overt emphasis upon walking with God in the here and now.

For some time this "right now" theology seemed a curiosity to me. Yet over time I came to see the grace in it. God, who is superabundant in mercy, who always extends pardon to the contrite, desires that we walk with him anew today...right now.

Today is the right time to draw near God. Today is the day of grace. Today Christ is calling you to serve your neighbor. It is a well-known tradition of the Christian Brothers that when you hear the ringing of a bell, it is to remind us that we live in the holy presence of God. It is a reminder that we walk with him now, today. Their durable and concrete expressions of love moved me deeply on more than a few occasions. Yes, this Catholic community butted heads. They stumbled, struggled, and sometimes failed, but it also modeled that real family members who live in the presence of God do not give up on each other. Catholics view the Body of Christ as a huge family—not a metaphorical family, not a symbolic family, but a real flesh-and-blood family. The Catholic Church is truly a divinely created family bound together by Christ's own flesh and blood. It's the mystical body of Christ.

A Christian Brother shared with me a wonderfully simple yet challenging perspective on evangelism. It made a deep impression upon me. He said, "There are two ways we Brothers share our faith. The first way is to, as quietly and as faithfully as possible, live out the Gospel with our lives. The second way is to speak the Gospel with our words. The second way is easy, anyone can speak—it's the first way that offers the greater challenge." They truly believe actions speak louder than words. While I had the immense privilege of visiting the Brothers' worldwide residence in Rome, there were Brothers there from all over the world. No one spoke to me about their faith. They didn't have to—I saw it in every move they made.

I observed that my Catholic friends did differ in some noteworthy ways. I was struck by the way they empathized with their brothers or sisters who had stumbled or failed morally. They were patient and caring toward one another during times of painful moral failure, rather than simply distancing themselves from the latest wrongdoer. There was a beautiful lack of judgment or condescension. As a pastor, more than a few times, I had sadly witnessed Christians turn their backs on one another during a person's greatest moment of need because of a drug problem, a sexual transgression, the waywardness of a child, a shameful financial collapse, or a messy firing at work. Sadly, these events often marked the moment when the wounded one began looking for another church home, another denomination, or stopped going to worship altogether.

It's not so easy to walk away in the Catholic family. I learned from my Catholic friends that a real family stands in fierce solidarity and helps one another through the extraordinarily difficult times of life. A real family hunkers down and sticks it out. I will be forever grateful for their witness. This community inspired me, and my family is much stronger for that. Am I saying Catholics do this perfectly? Of course not—that would be ludicrous. But as a pattern, the love I saw was durable, tenacious in its loyalty, and it did not blush at the funky messiness of life's lowest moments. I saw this up close and I experienced it personally. I saw a faith rooted and defended by the Church through the ages, a faith durable yet gracious, a faith freighted in mystery and still engaged with the real grit of this world, a faith that rolled up its tired sleeves and expressed itself through genuine acts of love. Faith in Jesus Christ calls for compassion, and compassion always calls for action. Perfect? No. Beautiful? Absolutely. What I witnessed was a powerful and unvarnished apologetic to the truth of the gospel.

I also witnessed a love for the Bible while at Christian Brothers. During my lunch periods at the school I often found myself with another teacher or two, eating a sandwich, bent over the Bible in lively discussion. I've heard some say Catholics don't know the Bible. I know some Episcopalians, Methodists, Presbyterians, Lutherans, Jews, and Baptists who don't particularly know their Bible, either. Not long ago I was on a homily preparation committee at a local parish church. This group of Catholic laity met with the priest weekly to discuss and assist him with insights as he prepared his homily for the next Sunday—a brilliant idea. We would pray, read the appropriate passages, and discuss these texts for that liturgical week. We would discuss the meaning of the passage, its place in salvation history, and its practical applications for life. I was impressed by the reverence, depth of insight, and hermeneutic understanding of these lay persons. Not long ago I attended a wonderful conference on spiritual growth at a local Catholic church, to which the parishioners were encouraged to bring their Bibles. As I watched all the attendees pile into the sanctuary, Bibles in hand, I could not help thinking about how I had so often misunderstood Catholicism.

I would like to thank my Catholic friends at Christian Brothers High School who, during those exploratory days, patiently endured my endless questions, accepted me as a brother in Christ, and offered me an honest, unflinchingly accurate place to watch you live out your Catholic identity. The way you live matters and it is changing the world.

All through my life some of the people who have meant the most to me have been Catholic. The one at the very top of my list is Rosie (whom my kids love to call YaYa). In my opinion, she should be canonized. Funny how, when we were being pulled in every direction in the Protestant ministry, she was ministering powerfully to me and my family. She was a genuine expression of God's love and grace in my life during a stressful time. She loved me and my family like her own. What would I have done without her love?

I recently went to see her with one of my babies (now over six feet tall) and we brought her some lunch. We hadn't seen her in years. When we pulled up in the driveway she was at the door, waiting. She cried as we walked up and hugged our necks and kissed us like she always had. We had a wonderful lunch, reminiscing about old times: how we scared her with a plastic snake in the drawer not realizing she really had a dreadful fear of snakes…how our daughter would dress her up and put make-up all over her…how our boys would curl up beside her and make her watch Disney movies repeatedly… how I would decide to rearrange furniture and recruit (force) her to help me! Those were good times.

One thing she shared with us at that lunch was that she prayed for our family, each one by name, every night! The fact that she would pray for us daily was staggering to me. Rosie selflessly lived out her faith—a faith characterized by action, beauty, and love. I realized that day when we left that she is one of the reasons I am a Catholic.

station nine

a beautiful marriage

While I was in seminary, we lived in a thoroughly Italian Chicago neighborhood. All of our neighbors were Catholics. One evening, a neighbor we didn't yet know came to our humble apartment, bringing us some homemade manicotti she had just made. It was wonderfully delicious. I never said this, but I remember thinking privately that the gesture might actually be a self-serving act—bringing food to a poor seminarian and his wife in order to lay another cobblestone of good works to pave her way to heaven. Some non-Catholics might argue that these types of acts by Catholics may actually be self-serving deeds because they are a means to earn salvation through good works. At one point in my past I used to think Catholics actually believed this. Yes, I understood that grace was somehow involved in the mix, but it was up to Catholics to clinch the deal through good works. Now I feel ashamed at having even entertained such a thought. But somehow, somewhere it was communicated to me that at the core of Catholicism is a system of works-based righteousness. I was wrong. It takes only a cursory study of Catholicism to understand that the elect are saved by God's grace through the work of Jesus Christ, not by a system of human effort. Believing otherwise is one of the most persistent and damaging Protestant misunderstandings of Catholicism. Even a plain reading of Thomas Aquinas's "On the Necessity of Grace" in his momentous

Summa Theologica, reflects the Catholic position that salvation is all of grace, and that any responses or efforts to serve or please God are by that same grace. Aquinas asks:

> *Without grace can man know anything? Without God's grace, can man do or wish any good? Without grace, can man love God above all things? Without grace can man keep the commandments of the law? Without grace, can he merit eternal life? Without grace, can man prepare himself for grace? Without grace, can he rise from sin? Without grace, can man avoid sin? Having received grace, can man do well and avoid sin without any further Divine help? Can he of himself persevere in good?*

Aquinas's answer and the Catholic answer to each of these questions is unequivocally *No.* Our salvation, start to finish, is all by God's grace.

Where, then, do works fit into the Catholic scheme of salvation? This is where the gulf between Protestants and Catholics is tragically more linguistic than actual. It might shock some Protestants to know that, in recent history Pope Benedict XVI said, "Luther's expression *Sola Fide* is true if faith is not opposed to charity, to love" (Wednesday Audience, Nov. 19, 2008). Is the Pope contradicting the Council of Trent which proclaimed, "If anyone says that the godless are justified by faith alone…let him be anathema." (Trent, VI, chapter 7)? How can these two thoughts be reconciled? Answer: The same way Protestants hold in tension the teaching of Paul, who said, "We are saved by grace, not by works, so that no man can boast" and the teaching of James proclaiming that "faith without works is dead."

Catholics understand this tension just as Protestants do. Good works testify to our justification—they are not themselves that justification. Luther held to this, Calvin held to this, Aquinas held to this, Augustine held to this, as did Pope Benedict XVI and the Catholic Church. Even the most ardent Calvinist who embraces *Sola Fide,* justification by faith alone, needs to clarify this credo. A person may verbally claim to be justified by faith alone. But if there is in reality no concern for the things of God, no inclination toward service to Christ, and that person bears absolutely no fruit of good works, this individual's empty profession will not save him. We are indeed justified by faith alone—a faith that follows and serves Christ.

Even today, as I attended Mass, a prayer was offered: "O God, who through the grace of adoption chose us to be children of light…" Catholics look to the God of mercy and grace for their salvation—not to their own works. A beautiful Eucharistic prayer echoes: "You (Lord) constantly offer pardon and call on sinners to trust in your forgiveness alone." Though the language differs between Catholics and Protestants, it's all about grace. In my observation, many Protestants have a tendency to lean toward focusing upon and celebrating their justification (not to the exclusion of their sanctification, of course), whereas Catholics have a proclivity to stress and celebrate the ongoing process of sanctification (not to the exclusion of their justification).

All would agree that faith in Jesus Christ is preeminent, obedience to his will is a necessary expression of true faith, and the gift of eternal life is all by grace. I believe all would surely embrace the final words of St. Therese of Lisieaux, the Little Flower, who, on her deathbed, confessed, "Everything is grace. Everything is grace." To this we can all say, *Amen*!

Catholicism promotes a spirituality with a far more integrated understanding of faith and charity than I had previously considered. True faith necessarily manifests itself through good works, and good works are a confirmation, the happy fruit of genuine, living faith. Again, most informed Protestants would absolutely agree. As one reads the parable of the sheep and the goats in the twenty-fifth chapter of the Gospel of Matthew, one encounters the sobering separation of the righteous and the unrighteous at the end of time. This was some very straight-talk by Jesus. In this parable Jesus taught that those individuals who display acts of love and charity are ushered into eternal life, while those who do not show acts of mercy and kindness toward others face divine justice. Does this passage teach that we merit eternal life through our works or personal efforts? Absolutely not: The acts of mercy reflected in this passage are markers of genuine faith, evidence of the spiritual condition of a person's heart. Catholics take this teaching seriously—as should every Christian. Good works, deeds of charity, are where faith and action embrace. Protestant or Catholic, a profession of faith with no good works, with no expression of compassion, is but empty confession. St. James calls this type of faith *dead*. True spirituality produces a beautiful marriage of faith and action.

Not only are good works a manifestation of genuine faith, but works can also encourage increased faith. Theologically, this thought can make some Protestants nervous, out of the fear of external legalism, but in fact, we understand this and generally live this way. This is why husbands bring flowers to their wives even though they might not hold particularly romantic feelings that day. It is why we go to worship even though we might feel God is distant. *And it's why* we teach our children to say *thank you* even though they are five years old and have yet to grasp fully the notion of gratitude. Doing the right thing is good and can often encourage further faithfulness. The Catholic Church understands, as do most people, that sometimes we change from the outside in.

The Catholic Church encourages good works not as a means to earn one's salvation, but as an expression of true faith and to encourage increasing faithfulness. Many people mistake the "rules" of the Catholic Church—fasting, saying the rosary, crossing oneself, observing Lent, going to confession, etc.—as legalism rather than as ways to build healthy habits that encourage faith. Can good works slip into legalism? Of course they can, whether you're Catholic, Methodist, Baptist, or Presbyterian. It's an issue of the heart. This should never hinder us, though, from heeding the exhortation from the author of Hebrews, to "spur one another on to love and good deeds."

Now to a confession I wish I didn't have to make…Years ago I believed as a Protestant that somehow I had a better grasp of the gospel, a fuller, deeper understanding of grace, than did my Catholic friends—as if the Reformation had supplied me with a lens allowing me greater biblical clarity and insight. It's embarrassing to acknowledge I believed this. But I did. Now I grasp the immense egotism of this. Yet I still see this notion implicitly communicated in various ways, subtle and not, within the Protestant world. I have heard such sentiments from fellow Protestants, as if Catholics wouldn't be Catholics anymore if they just understood the gospel "rightly."

Since embracing Catholicism, I've heard similar comments addressed to me: *I thought you really understood grace. I thought you really knew the Gospel. I have heard you preach so many times, do you not believe in grace anymore?* As if one couldn't simultaneously grasp the full weight of the gospel of grace and be a dedicated Catholic.

It's been my experience that most Catholics are very longsuffering and rather tight-lipped with non-Catholics about these kinds of statements. I have also come to regard such remarks—that somehow Protestants get grace right and Catholic don't—as less than benevolent. Mutual love and charity calls for all of God's children to celebrate filial love and our union in Christ.

Catholics not only understand the gospel, but have thoroughly challenged me to live it out in the world where the rubber of faith meets the road of reality. Catholicism affirms that following Christ is much more than uttering a "sinner's prayer" or adhering intellectually to a corpus of doctrines. James warns us that "even the demons believe and tremble." Faith is not just about mere notional gospel, or belief in a theology, or gaining access into heaven. It is, rather, a call to love God, to love our neighbor, and to follow practically in Christ's footsteps of sacrificial service. Faith and works are so organically interconnected that we cannot pull them apart. Works are an outward sign of inward reality.

This is the beautiful message of Jesus' Sermon on the Mount. The love of true saving faith radiates from a believer's life in tangible ways. Like Jesus, we are to take up a towel and basin and lovingly wash feet. From a biblical perspective, there is never a disconnect between loving Christ and serving him. Through faith in Christ and through joining ourselves to his body in the Eucharist, which was given to us by Jesus himself, we move progressively into the divine life of love. To know God is to love, and to love God is to serve. Faith in Christ and service to him form a seamless garment.

The Catholic Church is thoroughly, wonderfully challenging in this regard. The gospel leads us to live out our faith in the messy trenches of life—to love and forgive people who hate us, to pray for those who are the enemies of God, to help unwed mothers, to engage unpopular issues regarding social justice and economic oppression, to defend the poor, to address difficult topics such as modern slavery, child labor abuses, and the sex trade.

When my daughter returned from helping the poor in Mozambique, she reported things to me that no one should ever have to endure. Yet we as God's people must roll up our sleeves and serve those who suffer. We are to do the hard, costly work of educating those in need so that they can one day be able to supply for themselves and their families. We are to deliver healing to those who live in sickness, to feed the hungry, to serve those who live in misery as the result of war and political strife. Costly, dangerous, politically messy, and personally inconvenient as this work involves, it is what Christ has called his people to do. If Jesus can leave heaven to help us in our misery, we can serve others in need as well.

The gospel incarnate also compels us to do the difficult work of confronting unjust social structures, ecological abuse, corporate greed, and unpopular issues associated with our legal system. The implications of the gospel—lived out, rather than stored in our heads—also call us to simple, practical everyday responses: a gracious smile, prayerful patience, picking up a piece of litter, offering a kind word, helping a person with a chore, encouraging a child, sharing some money, or buying someone a meal.

When Mother Teresa was awarded the Nobel Prize for Peace, she was asked what can be done to bring about world peace. Her answer was profoundly simple and thoroughly Catholic: "Go home and love your family."

Certainly, the Catholic Church has experienced its share of struggles, difficult chapters, and embarrassments. Yet it has nonetheless faithfully persevered and stands unparalleled in its willingness to wade into the hardest human circumstances around the globe to offer light and life. No other single group in the history of the world has sought to do as much good for mankind. In Memphis for many years, nuns were never charged a fee as they stepped onto buses or trolleys. This custom arose from civic gratitude: Over fifty nuns had willingly sacrificed their lives serving the sick during the yellow fever epidemic that brought Memphis to its knees in 1878.

Or take the Notre Dame-educated Jesuit Bill Tomes, who for almost twenty years has ministered to young people in some of the toughest housing projects in Chicago. He can be seen today patrolling the dark, graffiti-marked hallways of the projects in his faded denim habit. When shooting breaks out among hostile gangs, this servant positions himself between the rival factions until the shooting stops. He has done this over fifty times. He places his own life in danger to save the lives of others.

Or take Catholic priest and army chaplain Captain Father Emil Kapaun who, while wounded by a grenade, continued to assist the wounded and allowed himself to be taken as a prisoner of war by the North Koreans to ensure that his men would not be massacred. In the POW camp he provided spiritual leadership, worked to improve conditions, and negotiated for food. It was said that he saved hundreds

Army Captain Fr. Emil Kapaun.

of lives. While in the camp, as a result of cruel treatment, he died of pneumonia on May 23, 1951. He was buried in a mass grave near the Yalu River.

Then there is Father Damien. As a young missionary to the Hawaiian Islands in 1873, he learned of a leper colony on the island of Moloka'i. The lepers, all social outcasts, lived in undignified squalor. Seeing this tragedy, he asked permission to be permanently located to the leper colony.

Father Damien, known as "the Apostle to the Lepers," built new houses, constructed a school, and raised a church for these forgotten people. He attended to their medical needs as best he could. Knowing this day would probably come, Father Damien finally contracted the dreaded Hansen's disease. He gathered his congregation and told them, "My fellow lepers, I am now one of you." He faithfully served the colony until his death from leprosy-related complications. He sacrificially lived the incarnational love of Jesus.

These are just a few of the wealth of stories across the millennia of service and sacrifice as a result of the Catholic Church's presence in every corner of the world. These stories might seem extreme, but they are no more extreme than what Jesus did for us. This is precisely what Jesus meant when he said, "If anyone desires to come after me, he must deny himself, take up his cross and follow me." Without the presence of the Catholic Church in the world, our planet would be a different, much darker place. Genuine faith produces good works and it is God's plan that these acts of love change the world.

10

faith
and pizza

A former parishioner, struggling to understand my migration into the Catholic Church, asked, "What about everything you learned in seminary? What about what you believe? Have you abandoned these things?"

My answer: "No. I have not abandoned them. They have only been wonderfully enlarged, they have only been expanded. There has been no loss, only gain. You need to know that there is more." Peter Kreeft, author and professor at Boston College, who was a Calvinist before embracing Catholicism, once told a friend of mine, "When a Protestant becomes a Catholic it's like a Jew becoming a Christian. He becomes more Jewish— not less." Kreeft went on to say, "I regard myself as more of an evangelical now that I am a Catholic than I ever could be as a Protestant." I could not agree more.

My former parishioner pressed on: "Do you still believe in salvation by grace?"

"Yep."

"Do you still believe in the sovereignty of God?"

"Yep."

"Do you still believe the Bible is the authoritative Word of God?"

"Yep," I said. Then it was my turn, "Do you like pizza?"

"Yes, I love pizza," she said. "Why?"

I continued, "I love cheese and Italian sausage pizza. I'm always happy with a cheese and Italian sausage pizza."

She was making one of those what-does-this-have-to-do-with-anything faces. "Bear with me," I said. "My former ecclesiastical position was a tasty, hot, three-cheese pizza with Italian sausage—very nice. Yet the more I studied the Church fathers, the Eucharist, the saints, the church calendar, and the catholicity of the Church, the more I saw the Church as a huge, steaming, deep dish pizza piled high with all kinds of toppings—anchovies, artichokes, bell peppers, shrimp, mushrooms, Italian sausage, various cheeses, and some kind of sprinkles I'd never seen before. Even one piece is more than you could eat! You see, there's nothing lost—only wonderful things gained. Nothing forfeited—just much, much more pizza," I said. "That's what a doctorate in theology will get you!"

She got the message. Again, as Kreeft so accurately framed it, when a Protestant becomes a Catholic, it's rather like a Jew becoming a Christian, becoming not less Jewish but more. Embracing Catholicism has profoundly expanded—never reduced—my understanding of faith, the Church, the Eucharist, and service to Christ. Within the Catholic Church there are so many different orders, so many different rites, so much rich history, so much profound theology, an amazing calendar of feasts, so much outstanding literature, so much astonishing art, so much diversity, so many expressions of faith, so many ways to serve, that a person could spend a lifetime investigating but a tiny portion. Through a study of Renaissance artists I became enthralled with the frescos of Andrea Pozzo, an artist who painted a one-of-a-kind ceiling at the Church of St. Ignatius in Rome. His work with perspective was ground-breaking. While in Rome, I could easily have spent an entire afternoon just marveling at the ceiling.

Again, the "pizza" of the Catholic Church is huge, rich, steamy, deep, and delicious. Life is far too short to exhaustively experience it. Now, you might not like anchovies, or you might not have an affinity for bell peppers, but they are part of this incredibly complex pizza as well. When someone enters the Catholic Church, they embrace the whole pizza—not that the whole pizza is fully understood, and not that they don't struggle with various ingredients. Nonetheless, that sumptuously gigantic, wonderfully

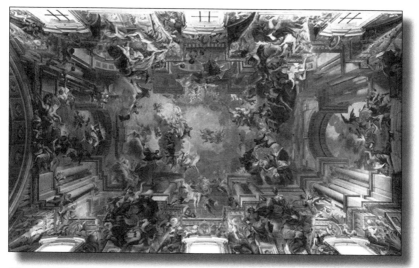

The magnificent ceiling by Andrea Pozzo at the Church of St. Ignatius, Rome.

complex pizza is now *theirs*. Just one piece alone is an amazing feast. While in Rome one afternoon I had the joy of having lunch with a wonderfully personable artist from Columbia who had earned her doctorate studying Michelangelo's work in the Sistine Chapel—a lifetime of study dedicated to just one relatively small room at the Vatican. This is a good illustration of how expansive, how deep, how rich the Catholic Church really is. The Sistine Chapel is not even one slice of the pizza. To stick with our metaphor, the Sistine Chapel is actually just a few pickled capers sprinkled on top of a single slice.

This next section may seem a bit heady. But hang in there—this is important. Another reason for the concept of *more* in Catholicism goes well beyond the enormous size of the Church's historical footprint. Some of its bigness finds its origin in Catholic thought and relates more to theology and logic. This was at first a curiosity to me. But I more and more began to grasp the beauty and challenge in this way of thinking. In a way, it runs against the grain of some tightly prescribed Western thought patterns. It is a "*both / and*" way of approaching things rather than an *either / or* paradigm. When you mention this to priests, deacons, brothers, nuns, or teachers of theology, they smile. This is part of the warp and woof of Catholic thought and pedagogy. Though statements at times and in certain relationships may appear to be contradictory, actually they often are not. Some people, in the world of logic and theology, call these apparent contradictions antinomies, things that at first glance appear to be inconsistent or contradictory, but in reality they have a unique relationship to one another. Years ago, I heard a truly sad story that well expresses this idea. A young man learned by phone that his wife had been in a two-car accident. She was injured, but she was going to be fine. Shortly after, he received another call informing him his wife had been killed in a collision between a car and a bus. Stunned as he hung up the phone, he was certain one of these stories had to be wrong. In reality, both stories were correct. His wife had been in a two-car collision, was injured, and as someone was racing her in their car to the emergency room, there was a second fatal collision with a bus. Things are not always as they first appear. Often there is more to the story.

In his classic work *Orthodoxy*, G.K. Chesterton, a convert to Catholicism, writes that Catholicism is thoroughly characterized by this *both/and* way of thinking. It gives wide margins for critical thought and consideration, rather than tightly-wrapped categories. Do we loathe sin, or do we love the sinner? *Yes*. Is Jesus fully God, or is he fully human? *Yes*. Is God sovereign, or are we free? *Yes*. Should we aid the poor, or wean them from dependency? *Yes*. Is God transcendent (beyond us), or is he immanent (near us)? *Yes*.

This element in Catholic thought provides a great deal of latitude, liberating believers from serving restrictive categories of thought. There is a wise symmetry, a prudent balance involved in this way of perceiving things. Can we know God through faith, or do we know him through reason? *Yes*. Might the end of history be soon, or might it be in the distant future? *Yes*. Does sin do violence to the victim, or does it injure the sinner? *Yes*. Should our faith be practical, or should it concern itself with mystery? *Yes*.

As a minister formerly in the Reformation tradition, I used to believe that tight, precise categories actually required deeper, more critical thinking. I have since found the exact opposite to be true. Tight, clearly delineated categories are actually easier on the thinker, requiring less effort because the categories themselves perform much of the intellectual heavy lifting. Broader notions kept in a tension and requiring thoughtful circumspection and balanced consideration often place a greater demand on the one who is doing the thinking. Is the priesthood for men alone, or should we fight diligently for the rights of women? *Yes.* Is human nature good, or is human nature sinful? *Yes.* I have found that as a result of this, Catholic thought can often be far more intellectually stimulating and epistemologically challenging than the well-trimmed categories of my theological past. This is why Catholicism can hold in tension so many various perspectives and theological considerations. It allows for broader reflections and encourages a healthy circumspection. This way of thinking is organically connected to the bigness of the Catholic Church.

I have not been able to put my finger on it yet, however much I have reflected, but there is also something wonderfully organic and intrinsically human about the Catholic faith. It fits our humanity. It resonates with the divine image. My son once said, "I really like being a Catholic, Dad."

I thought I knew what he was getting at, but I wanted to hear him express himself. "Why is that, son?"

"Because it fits like a comfortable old coat. It's roomy and just fits right." He is right—there is indeed something about Catholicism that just fits our humanity. When I mentioned this to a priest once, he just smiled. Catholicism resonates as true to the human experience. It offers a richness, a harmony, a texture, a thickness, a beauty that has grown from millennia of faith and human experience. Its art, architecture, poetry, literature and liturgy feeds one at the level of the secret soul.

As one reads the writings of the contemplatives, works by Thomas à Kempis, John of the Cross, Therese of Lisieux, Brother Lawrence, Thomas Keating, Basil Pennington, or Thomas Merton, one is moved by the authenticity, the genuine humanity of the their faith and struggles. They speak to the real condition of mankind in their personal encounters with God. Interestingly, many Protestant evangelicals are now reading the works of Catholic contemplatives because their writings speak in a way consonant with the human condition. It fits our humanity. Catholicism addresses the deepest longings of the human heart. It fosters a mystagogical imagination which ponders things seen and the unseen, taps into the liturgical rhythm of heaven, and boldly encourages tasting the goodness of God. Catholicism is aesthetically beautiful, intellectually challenging, metaphysically complex, globally embraced, and gives an unearthly peace to the human soul. It is strangely congruent with the way things are.

As the late Notre Dame professor John Howard Yoder wrote, "People who bear crosses are living with the grain of the universe." Catholicism encourages us, as sojourners upon this spinning world, to live with the grain of the universe.

The Catholic Church is so vast, diverse, and deep that you will run out of days before you can thoroughly explore it entirely. The Catholic tradition effectively affirms that we are fearfully and wonderfully made and faith, like music, speaks to the human soul. Yet, on a practical level, it promotes a faith that works. It is a worldwide body gathered from all the nations of the earth. Its theology is beautiful, optimistic, and encouragingly not so overly fixated on heaven that it overlooks the beauty and significance of the temporal. It cuts earnestly at the tap root of materialism, individualism, selfish nationalism, and secular pragmatism. It challenges one to adopt a global understanding and appreciation for world-wide art, culture, customs, and manners.

To be Catholic is to be always learning and globally tolerant. One day while praying at the Basilica di Santa Maria del Fiore in Florence, I was surrounded by people from every corner of the earth. These were my brothers and sisters. I did not speak their language but they showed filial kindness toward me. On another occasion, visiting the Church of St. Mary and the Angels, where St. Francis of Assisi stepped over into eternity, I spontaneously joined a large group of Russian pilgrims. Though I do not speak Russian, I knew they were saying the Lord's Prayer. I was immediately accepted into their group and knelt with them for prayer as if they were parish friends from my old neighborhood. As we finished the prayer, I received a friendly pat on the back as a gesture of kindness from someone I had never met, from the other side of the earth. The Catholic Church by its very nature transcends time, language, economic theory, social status, nationalism, and cultural barriers.

Once, before I left for a mission trip to Cuba, a Protestant elder confronted me. "Why would you want to go there? They are communist."

For a moment I thought silence might be the most appropriate response. But I simply replied, "Because the Church is really big and we have brothers and sisters there." He had not considered how his faith might extend beyond his patriotic, political, or geographic concerns. Catholics know they are part of a truly vast family.

Catholicism speaks to us as spiritual, intellectual, and physical beings, and in doing so engages the whole person. My first Easter vigil in the Catholic Church was personally an astounding experience as I brought my candle into the darkness of the worship space, darkness ushered in by the solemnity of Good Friday. The sweetness of the incense, the sprinkling of holy water, the retelling of the covenants of God, rich prayers from across the centuries, the naming of faithful saints of history, the physicality of making the sign of the cross, the visual power of the liturgy—all gave honor to Christ while simultaneously engaging all our human senses. Catholicism speaks powerfully to what it means to be a human person.

I think at this point in our journey, I am in. I really love all I'm learning about the Catholic Church. I don't understand it all, but remember coming from my neat and tidy doctrinal background- I appreciate that I cannot explain it all. God is as mysterious as is his Church. Who are we to think we can figure it all out and explain it all? I'm good with that! I have to watch myself because I am so excited and I want to tell everyone we are Catholic and Durant is trying to be more diplomatic—as always. We are going to the Catholic Church and in fact, I have even gone to Mass in the middle of the week, by myself—a miracle in itself!

Finally, when I was given permission to tell people that we were now Catholic, I ran into someone I'd gone to church with as a Protestant. She asked where we were going to church and I told her we had become Catholic. Her face wore a strange look. Then she said, "Oh, that's great. I think there are some Catholics who are probably Christians."

I smiled and replied, "I think there are some Protestants who are probably Christians too!"

Now, looking back, I know I shouldn't have tossed off that sarcastic reply. But the exchange does demonstrate the lack of knowledge people have about the Catholic Church and what we actually believe. Many people believe only what they are told—they haven't learned for themselves. Here's an example…

Durant used to conduct a lot of weddings. When he left the house he would say, "I'm going to marry somebody. I'll be back later." One evening when Durant was leaving the house to go "marry somebody," our daughter, then aged four or five, curiously asked, "Daddy, when are you going to bring your other wives home? You marry all these people, but when are you going to bring them home?" She simply believed exactly what she'd been told.

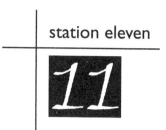

table talk

I shared some of my findings with a Catholic friend over dinner. He also holds a master's in theology and was graciously willing to endure an avalanche of questions. I told him it was a great practical comfort to know we have a cloud of witnesses, of believers who have gone before us, who are in heaven pulling for us as we struggle along our earthly pilgrimage. We are not divorced from those in the faith who have died—they are alive and well and we are all still united in Christ.

He smiled, knowing I was referring to the communion of saints. It is a great mystery, what the saints know and how they are engaged with the dealings of this world. But they are a beautiful encouragement and inspiration to us who still walk this earth. These are profound mysteries of the faith. As St. Dominic lay dying, those around him wept in grief of the eminent loss of this great leader. Seeing their grief, he comforted them. "Do not weep, for I shall be more useful to you after my death and I shall help you then more effectively than during my life." Those who have died have not ceased to exist—they are just elsewhere. Just as when a loved one goes away on a great trip, they are not annihilated—they are just elsewhere and we continue to love them and pray for them.

When a person comes into the Catholic Church they take a confirmation name, usually the name of a saint who means something special to them. As an educator, I took the confirmation name John Baptist de LaSalle, founder of the Christian Brothers and patron saint of teachers. I have studied his life and mission for years, but if you were to ask me

Sharon and I celebrating our journey and Confirmation names, Cecilia and John Baptist de LaSalle.

why I selected this name I would just have to say that our paths have crossed in a number of personal, mysterious, and meaningful ways. The communion of saints is a beautifully encouraging aspect of Catholicism. The saints have much to teach us. A wonderful way to become more involved with the communion of saints is to begin reading and celebrating the biographies of their lives on their respective feast days. For example, as I write this, yesterday was the feast day of the Irishman, St. Oliver Plunkett, today is the feast of St. Thomas the Apostle, and tomorrow is the feast of St. Elizabeth of Portugal. Each day offers another opportunity to meet another member of our worldwide family and to be encouraged by their life and faith. Studying the saints each day, we connect with our heritage and are inspired by those who have run the race before us and eagerly wait for us to join them one day.

The dinner conversation with my friend shifted to the curious topic of purgatory. This issue is really no great leap for a student of the Bible. Paul makes it clear that after death, we will experience a purifying. This notion is not unique to Catholicism. I believed this as a Presbyterian minister. All Christians who know their Bible know that Paul taught in the third chapter of his Epistle to Corinth that "fire will test the quality of each man's work" (1 Cor. 3:13). Quality works of gold, silver and precious stones will endure, whereas the wood, hay, and stubble of our lives will be burned away as we pass from this life and into the presence of God. This is a biblically-based reality. Once, as I led a Bible study at a Protestant church on this particular text, a participant reacted, "Isn't that Catholic?" I re-read the text and then asked him how he came to the conclusion that this portion of Scripture was just for Catholics.

Another misunderstanding is that purgatory is a *place*. This idea gained traction after Dante published his *Divine Comedy*. Purgatory is not a place, not a piece of real estate. It is that purifying *process* that every believer will experience as she or he is brought into the presence of a perfect and all-holy God. This purifying "as if by fire" happens in eternity, which is *outside* of time. Perhaps it's instantaneous, perhaps not. We do not know—it's in eternity.

As well, nowhere does the Catholic Church teach that purgatory is a place for "second chances," where souls who have rejected the offering of God's salvation in life can rethink the issue, repent, believe, and thus be saved. No, the purifying journey is reserved for those who have been granted eternal life and are on their way, being prepared for the banquet feast of the Lamb. Simply put, purgatory is the beautification of the bride preparing to meet the groom. As a pastor officiating scores of weddings, I had the privilege before the wedding of venturing into the semi-sacred space of the bridal chamber, where brides were being prepared for their grooms. This is an earthly foreshadowing of the believer's preparation to see Christ, the groom of the Church. I have been encouraged by the Catholic Catechism, which teaches that this part of our journey is not to be feared, remembering (as the ancients used to say), *Deus Pro Nobis*— "God is for us." This is a magnificent mystery, something for which Catholicism leaves a great deal of room.

Then the conversation with my friend shifted again. I told him I had found that if anyone in the history of the Church truly has a heart for Christ and his Church, it has to be his mother Mary. I mused as a curious non-Catholic, "Her entire life was utterly surrendered to the loving and sacrificial support of her son." He looked at me as if I had struck a melodious chord. "No one could be more dedicated or sympathetic to the work of Jesus than his mother," I added. I discovered this to be true not only in ecclesiastical history, but in my own private experience. I do not consider myself to be a mystic, but my path, in sometimes curious ways, had crossed with Mary, especially during times of fear, pain, uncertainty, or hardship. I pulled out my smart phone and showed my friend a beautiful image of Mary painted by the sixteenth century artist Sassoferrato. "I love this painting."

He seemed surprised, "Where did you get that?!"

It was strange, I told him. No one had encouraged me to carry this picture. It was not some evangelistic gift as an effort to convert me. I told him, "Mary just seems to be near at times…this painting, well, it brings me peace. I can't explain it. Strangely, it brings me joy." I smiled and just for fun sang that familiar refrain from the Beatles, "When I find myself in times of trouble, Mother Mary comes to me…"

My dinner guest leaned forward in his chair, laughed, and jested, "You are a Catholic, my friend! When Mary shows up and comforts you, you're done. You *are* Catholic!" We both laughed aloud. I wasn't sure what all this exactly meant at the time, but we were both wiping away tears because we knew it was true.

Now I genuinely was a Catholic…I just didn't know it yet. Sometimes it works that way. More than a few times, I'd asked the Holy Spirit to help me and to show me the way. Interestingly, as I continued to study the ancient Church, I found myself more and more inclined toward the liturgy. It rests upon the historical foundation of the early Church, it is anchored to a balanced scriptural calendar, and it relies very little upon the personality or whims of a pastor. I began reading curiously about the historical role of Mary, who has been all but expunged from some Protestant traditions. (As an aside, note that Martin Luther's devotion to Mary far surpasses that of modern-day Protestantism.) Mary was universally honored by the early Church. In some church circles today, though Mary is almost a taboo subject, we must admit: There was hardly anyone else in salvation history who could be said to be her equal. Mary fulfilled a role no one else will ever replicate. I confess I knew very little about Mary, yet I learned that, throughout the history of the Church, Mary has held many titles. She has been referred to as the New Eve, the one who crushed the head of the serpent, the first disciple of Christ, and Mother of the Church. Her role has always been to direct the nations to follow her son. Her last recorded words in Scripture, spoken at the wedding of Cana, were, "Do whatever he (Jesus) tells you to do" (Jn.

2:5). This has been her role ever since, to advance the ministry of her son Jesus. Catholic theologians often say that any honor she receives is merely reflected honor, just as the moon reflects light from the brilliance of the sun. As I studied this unparalleled character of faith, the mother of Jesus, I began to see how she was wonderfully prefigured by the Ark of the Covenant, the holiest object in the old covenant. The Ark of the Covenant, which represented the presence of God, contained the words of God on tablets of stone, the staff of the high priest, and a portion of the miraculous bread, manna. These were shadows of realities to come. It was Mary who faithfully carried within her body Jesus, who was and is the Word of God, our great high priest, and the bread of life. Mary is the only human being in the New Testament to speak to and engage an archangel of God. It was Gabriel who reveals that Mary was indeed full of grace. Her humility, her obedience to God, and her unwavering support of her son's ministry stands as a model for humble faith and unwavering discipleship. The Magnificat in scripture describes it all. By bringing Jesus into the world, Mary became the Mother of the Church.

In the fourth century, Cyril of Alexandria became involved in a church scuffle with a heresy called Nestorianism. Nestorianism advanced the view that Jesus had two distinct natures, denying the perfect union of his divine and human nature, and thereby undermining the fullness of the Incarnation—theologically, a very big deal indeed. Those who adhered to this heresy refused to call Mary the accepted title of *Theotokos* ("mother of God"), but rather referred to Mary with the subtly reduced title of *Christotokos* ("mother of Christ"). If you know your creeds you know the outcome...the ancient understanding of the Incarnation and the acceptance of the title *mother of God* was defended and affirmed at the Council of Ephesus (AD 431). This constituted a supreme council of the entire church. Mary, as defended by the Church, is the Mother of God. In John's Apocalypse, Mary is forever honored by her son in heaven, hence given the ancient title *Queen of Heaven* (Rev. 12: 1). As Mary's heart was torn by the rejection and death of her son, as foretold by Simeon, so she is universally viewed as the icon of sympathy, compassion, and patient understanding during times of grief and distress.

Many wrongly believe that Catholics worship Mary. If a Catholic—

or anyone else, for that matter, be they Baptist, Methodist, Presbyterian, Episcopalian, or Quaker—worships Mary, they are out of accord with the teachings of Scripture and the Church. Worship is reserved for God alone. As was referenced earlier, I have come to discover that most Protestants do not reject the Catholic Church. Rather, what they reject is a *misrepresentation* of it. This is often so true on the subject of Mary. She is an unparalleled figure in salvation history who has been highly honored since the time of the Apostles.

As I spoke with my friend over dinner I was reminded of the two disciples on the road to Emmaus who walked with Jesus and exclaimed, "Were not our hearts burning within us as he spoke." On that memorable evening I found my heart, time and time again, was deeply stirred as we discussed these things. My heart was only confirming what I had come to be known as true within my head.

In my many visits with priests (most of them unbelievably patient) I have come to understand that Catholicism truly believes that in the providence of God we are all at different places in our spiritual journeys and that this in itself is truly a beautiful thing. Wherever you are in life, God understands and loves you superabundantly. Catholicism gives you the freedom to be who you are, right where you are, on your unique pilgrimage. This reality is handled by clergy and parishioners with dignity and care. Your one-of-a-kind journey with Christ is a unique work of art produced by the Holy Spirit, and is intimately and ultimately between you and God. It is wonderfully refreshing to come just as you are, on your distinctive sojourn, with diverse brothers and sisters from all over the planet and from across the millennia, to meet with the God who made you, who loves you deeply, and who by grace is herding us home.

Now remember, Durant is my forger, and he does the heavy lifting when it comes to theological study. I watched him plow right through a thousand pages of the Catechism of the Catholic Church, and without missing a beat move on to the next book. I knew he was on to something and he wouldn't let go.

All this reading started getting expensive! As we learn more about the Catholic Church I become more joyful and excited. It has brought a peace into our home. The Catholic Church also brought us mystery. As I have been married for almost three decades, raised three children, dealt with personal pain and struggles in life, as we all do, I have come to realize that life generally is not organized into neat, explainable categories. Life is not black and white, cut and dried—there are real mysteries. Our God is mysterious. There is more about God that we don't know than we know. There is more about heaven that we don't know than we do know. I don't have, nor do I need, all the answers. I now began to see the mystery of the faith, the beauty of the Church, and I appreciated those things that didn't necessarily fit into the tidy boxes of my past. I distinctly remember coming home the day when I understood more about what the communion with the saints really means. I cried. This was huge for me.

My mother died when I was only seventeen. I was told by a minister that she was gone, that I could not talk to her or see her again until that one day when I, too, went to heaven. For years this had caused me great pain. It was as if I was divorced from her in the sense that our relationship was done for now. The Catholic understanding of the communion of saints taught me something very different, very comforting. The dead are not amputated from the living. No, the fellowship continues. The living and those in heaven form one Church, the mysterious body of Christ, and just as we pray for and encourage one another in life, we also do in death. We are still one body in communion. Death does not change this. If a loved one were to take a long trip to a place far away, would we stop praying with and for them, or would we stop loving them? I remember standing by my bed and telling Durant that I felt as if I had been robbed of years of peace. Now I know not only that my mother is in heaven, but that I can speak to her, pray with her and she for me. I am encouraged by the Church to ask her and the saints to help me, to intercede for me before the throne of God. Do Catholics worship the dead? Absolutely not. Do Catholics believe that our love for one another and our spiritual fellowship is unbroken by death? Absolutely. I had not "lost" my mother—she was just fine and is interceding for me even now.

I was so glad to learn that I could turn to Mary, Jesus' mother, as well as to all of my spiritual family in heaven, and join with them in prayer and praise to the Lord our God. How beautiful and how comforting! Why had I not ever been told that? This was life-changing. The more I understood the role of Mary, Mother of the Church, the more comforted I was. It changed me from someone who had walked around for over twenty years without a mother, to having two!

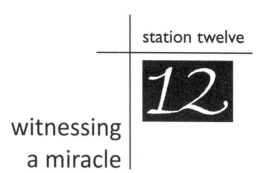

station twelve

witnessing
a miracle

One Saturday afternoon, I asked my Catholic dinner guest friend whether he were going to Mass that weekend. He assured me he was. Taking a step of faith, I imposed a little and whether I might attend with him. Without raising an eyebrow, or asking a single question, I found myself, an ordained Presbyterian minister, being driven to a Catholic Mass.

As I have already mentioned, I have since discovered that Catholics firmly believe in the providence of God in the life of each individual. There is a bold trust that God really knows what he is doing. Everyone has their own journey, and in a freeing way, it's really no one else's business, it's a sacred thing. So as we drove, my friend just let it be. That in itself was a very beautiful thing. As we quietly entered the sacred space, I whispered a confession to my friend, "I really do not want to offend anyone, but I am not sure what to do…the crossing, kneeling, holy water, standing, bowing…" He simply replied, "No worries…Just watch and pray."

Having professionally planned and led countless worship services over the decades, I was unprepared for what I was about to experience. As we sat a couple rows from the back, on the right side facing the altar, I picked up on a real sense of anticipation. You could feel it—it was tangible. Yes, people quietly greeted one another, there were smiles and warm welcomes, yet there was this feeling of anticipation. The parishioners were *ready*. I wasn't sure for what, but I could tell they were ready for something. When the Mass began, everything shifted gears. The soft voices stopped. The welcomes ceased. All attention was focused upon the priest. *These people really are here to worship*, I thought.

I quickly noticed the volume of biblical texts that were being read. It surprised me. There was an Old Testament reading, antiphonal singing of a Psalm, another text read from an Epistle which was followed by an extensive Gospel reading. Great reverence was shown as everyone stood, sang, and made the sign of the Cross in preparation for the reading of Christ's sacred words. As the Mass unfolded, I became more and more taken aback by what I was experiencing—it was a beautiful convergence of biblical types, signs, allusions, songs, symbols, images, and phrases. It took the full weight of my theological understanding to keep up with the Mass: a quote from Malachi, a reference to John's Apocalypse, a phrase from Luke, a reference to Isaiah, a musical allusion to John the Baptist, a gesture from the earliest Church, the mention of Melchizedek, a prayer from the Psalms, a quote by an angel, and the challenging words of Christ himself. Quickly I realized I was witnessing century on century of theologically informed, carefully crafted worship. This was a spiritually-freighted experience developed across the millennia by the saints, led by the Holy Spirit.

I watched as this community made the sign of the cross as personal prayer and as an outward sign of dedication to our triune God. This ancient sign is as old as Christianity itself. Tertullian wrote to encourage the continual making of the sign of the cross. Cyril of Jerusalem wrote, "Be the cross our seal, made with boldness with our fingers upon our brow." This simple sign has been performed by billions of followers of Christ across history—by nuns serving in hospitals, school children before prayer, soldiers before battle, chaplains over the dying, lay people as they pass a hospital, monks in hiding, servers in soup kitchens, grandmothers saying the rosary, and families around the dinner table.

For many martyrs, the sign of the cross would be their last act upon earth. This beautiful and ancient gesture of faith was tragically one of those too-easily drawn "lines of demarcation" during the Reformation. With this sign one could quickly identify one's theological allegiances during that troubled period. Some Protestant groups continued to make the sign of the cross, though most did not. Today the majority of the Church makes the sign of that cross, yet for many Christians this rich tradition was sadly one of those beautiful babies thrown out with the choppy Reformational bathwater.

For a quarter of a century, I had worked countless hours with my Protestant colleagues to fashion theologically rich and spiritually meaningful worship services. But none of our best efforts could approach the historical density, the biblical richness, the theological gravity, the aesthetic profundity of the Catholic Mass. I could not help noticing the allusions to ancient temple worship, echoes of the synagogue, and the Eucharistic fingerprints of the early Church. Biblically and historically, it was all overwhelming for this lover of church history. From Solomon's temple of Jerusalem, to songs from the heavenly scenes in Revelation given us by John, it was all there. The Mass spans all redemptive history, focusing on God's covenants and how they beautifully converge in the person and work of Christ. It was as if the ancient, the present, and the heavenly all converged together in a frozen, timeless moment. There was also reverent genius in the use of silence, extended moments of absolute silence, intentional, prolonged pauses, rare opportunities to be still before God. These pregnant moments were in no way rushed. Theologically, aesthetically, historically, metaphysically, it was much more than I could get my head around. A child could attend Mass and be encouraged, yet a seasoned theologian could never fully fathom its depths.

When the priest extended his hands above the elements and spoke the ancient words of invocation, the epiclesis, Greek for "calling down from on high," all extraneous movement stopped. The rustling of parishioners stopped. Parents tending to children stopped. Even the ambient noise stopped. Time itself stopped as the divine broke through. Jesus' familiar words from the Gospel of John came to my mind: "Whoever eats my flesh and drinks my blood has eternal life, and I will raise him up on the last day." I was well acquainted with this passage. Jesus had been teaching on the miracle of manna, then pointed to his own body and blood as our new manna, a new miracle upon which we are to feed.

This teaching was so hard to accept that many of Jesus' disciples no longer followed him, and Jesus let them go. He did not chase them down to explain that he was merely speaking in metaphorical terms, or that he was employing symbolic language. He was teaching that his followers will eat his flesh and drink his blood at the Eucharist. The Mass is not a memorial service which reflects fondly upon that first Lord's Supper in the upper room, nor is it a prayerful and grateful gaze back upon the cross, nor is it a celebration of a unique spiritual presence of Jesus during the service—it is all this and more. The Mass involves the two thousand year-old miraculous Eucharistic transformation of the elements of bread and wine into the actual body and blood of Christ.

As I witnessed this Mass, my mind raced back to seminary days and my study of Greek, specifically the word *parousia*. Many evangelicals, including me as a Presbyterian minister, translate this word as *coming*, with a fully-future emphasis in reference to Jesus' second coming. Sitting at that Mass, I recalled that *parousia* also means "presence," without a future dimension associated. Is Jesus present now, or will he be present in the future? *Yes.* Here, in this moment, in the Eucharist, Jesus was present with his people. My next thoughts were of Jesus' promise to his Church at the end of Matthew's Gospel: "Surely I am with you *always*, even to the end of time." I now understood the Eucharistic amazement found in the worship of those surrounding me and throughout the history of the Church.

I knew that from the earliest Church until today, the Catholic Church believed in the real presence of Christ in the Eucharist. As I attended this Mass I was confronted not only with the gravity of two thousand years of Church teaching and worship, but also with the unambiguous words of Jesus: "This is my body…this is my blood"—a teaching so mysterious and difficult to grasp that some of his followers left him. I learned in that moment that at the center of the Catholic Church is the Eucharist, and at the center of the Eucharist is the real presence of Jesus Christ with his Church. These theological realities began locking together in my mind. They began fitting together with the order, unity, symmetry, and beauty of the great rose window of Notre Dame, and I almost fell out of my pew.

Unless one grasps the miracle of the real presence of Christ in the Eucharist one may never understand the rationale behind the grandeur of the great cathedrals of the world. The theological motivation for the staggering splendor and majesty of these awe-inspiring Cathedrals was to provide a proper frame for this miracle. As with a wedding ring, the Cathedral is the setting for the miraculous jewel of Christ's presence in the Eucharist. As I watched, I thought of the double miracle taking place. As the priest's hands covered the bread and wine, transformed

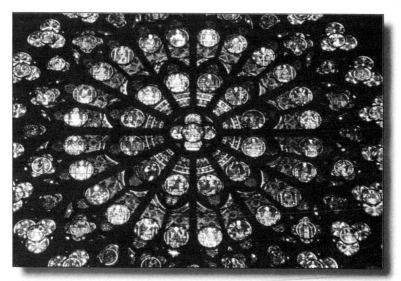

The Rose Window at Notre Dame, Paris.

by the Holy Spirit into the Body and Blood of Christ, so also by this meal Christ's people were being transformed into his mystical body, the Church, and as Peter taught, sharing even in his divine nature. This is the heart of Catholicism.

As the Mass ended, there occurred an extended moment of silence, then a short blessing by the priest. The parishioners crossed themselves, and a deacon exuberantly commissioned us all, "Go and announce the Gospel of the Lord!" With that, the congregation responded with a hearty "Thanks be to God!"

The Latin word for Mass, *missa*, means, "Go" or "Be sent," as on a mission. The end of the Eucharist marks the beginning of the believer's re-entry into the world as a missionary for Christ. The Mass in all of its beauty and profundity is not a retreat from the world, or divorced from things temporal. It actually transforms, equips, heals, empowers, and sends one back out onto the mission field of the real world again, and again, and again, and for the rest of our lives. The Mass continually calls God's people to be co-workers with Christ's in the world's redemption.

As I walked in silence across the parking lot after that Mass, I studied the ground intently. I knew what I was going to have to do. I was going to have to write a letter to my denomination and graciously inform them that my formal 25-year association with them had come to its end.

I no longer had any ground upon which to protest. I was following the ancient paths. I was going home.

One of the things I struggled with along my journey was the fact there would be a point when I would have to go to confession, also called the sacrament of reconciliation. Try confessing an entire lifetime of sins…it's not easy! This is hard for a life-long Protestant, as we are used to being "alone" with God and confessing in private. God forbid anyone else living should know all we have done.

Durant was smart enough to have his first confession while in Rome, on the other side of the world! Jokingly, he said he was going to try to find a priest who didn't speak English! I teased him about having to leave his own continent for his first confession, but secretly I wish I had, too. I knew I had to do it. When and where was the question. I had a week to go before entering the Church at the Easter Vigil Mass and was traveling on business in Long Island. I found a local Catholic Church. I think they were excited to have a first-timer. As I entered the confessional, I told the priest I was not really sure what to do and had never confessed to anyone but God-himself. I think I even said, "If I find out you've told anyone, I'm coming back for you!" He kindly told me not to worry. I got out my paper with everything I was supposed to say and got on with it. I went back as far as I could remember…

What happened to me that day was a gift from God. When I left, it was as if the weight of the world had been lifted off my shoulders! My feet were barely touching the ground. As I left that church that afternoon, they did something special I'll never forget: They rang the church bell for me!

I left knowing my sins were forgiven, and I wanted to go out and live my life as best as I could, not only to please God, but for my own good.

I don't want to have to go to a priest very often. I am sure I will sin again, but it does make you think twice since you know you have to go confess before you can take the Eucharist and I want to partake of the Eucharist as much as I can while I am living. It is nourishment for the soul. Not long ago, Durant and I attended a Mass. I remember watching with awe the beauty and mystery occurring at the altar. The Mass is centered upon the Eucharist, and at the Eucharist we are truly in the presence of God.

13

packing for no man's land

When a Protestant embraces Catholicism, it is usually not the product of one flash of insight, nor the result of one event that suddenly changes everything. Protestants generally don't become Catholics as the result of an especially persuasive personality or effective preacher. I have spoken with many Protestants who have made this journey. If you ask them how they became Catholic, they usually smile and say something like, "Now, that's a long story." They aren't joking. Often, it is a journey marked by time, careful reflection, misunderstandings by friends or family, intellectual challenge, and sometimes miracles. It is a highly personal experience they might not be willing to share.

Recently, I was speaking with a man who, while in deep reflection, heard the Holy Spirit speak to him, confirming the direction of his pilgrimage. He rarely ever speaks of this and was very guarded in telling me. During a festive reception, right after my wife and I came into the Church, I was approached by a chatty woman wearing cats-eye glasses. She had heard I was a former Presbyterian minister and asked quite frankly, with no introduction, "How did you become a Catholic?"

I smiled, took a sip of punch to buy time. General observation said she likely didn't want to hear a summary of my doctoral studies, or reflections on the Patristics' use of the word *Catholic*, or the historical significance of the real presence of Christ in the Eucharist, so I just said, "Now that's a long story. The Holy Spirit led me to His Church, and for that I am very grateful."

She understood that she was getting the shorthand story, but she also understood as a Catholic that this was how it usually works. The Holy Spirit leads a pilgrim on a sometimes daunting, unique and intimate journey hard to capture in mere conversation. Among those I have met who have become Catholics, the journey was not planned. It usually happened over a lengthy time. This usually was a rich time of wrestling and spiritual discovery, with deep joy, and the presence of the Holy Spirit.

Another common denominator I have found among those who have embraced Catholicism is that they experience a curious, unsettling period I call "No Man's Land." I am well acquainted with No Man's Land—it was my home for a while. In No Man's Land a Protestant begins to entertain the significance of many of the pre-Reformation positions in the Church. It is an eye-opener for some to understand that yes, there were fifteen centuries of faith and practice before Martin Luther nailed his 95 theses on the door at Wittenburg Cathedral. It is an eye-opener to some that the historical arc of the Catholic Church from the Apostles continues until today. It can be perplexing to learn that the historical center of gravity of the Church is actually Catholic. The majority of the Church through the ages is liturgical, has adhered to the real presence of Christ in the Eucharist, has acknowledged apostolic authority, makes the sign of the cross, honors Mary, and is Catholic. When one begins to understand this…begin packing.

Often, when Protestants first hear of these realities, they shut these thoughts down. I understand this reaction. They know they will have to entertain further questions. It will require some hard work and deep reflection, will produce some theological discomfort, and potentially may call for difficult personal decisions. I encountered all of these issues, plus the prospect of forfeiting my ordination as a Protestant minister.

Socially, there will be some friends and acquaintances who might never call again. For some, it is just so much easier not to go down this road. For those souls who do continue and begin to study these issues in depth, with the joy of discovery also comes a private No Man's Land. They are not Catholic, but the more they study, learn, and grow, the less reason they have to protest. They are, for this time, not fully a Protestant, not fully a Catholic. It's like dwelling in an ecclesiastical netherworld.

Many people who converted to Catholicism have shared with me that this was an extremely difficult time. Not entirely so, in my experience. I found this an invigorating period of exploration and growth. It was as if the tumblers of many years of study began falling into place before my eyes. Trinitarian spirituality, the superabundance of God's grace, the nature of conversion, the power of the Eucharist, the authority of the Church, and the global nature of the body of Christ—all these realities began to come into happy focus. Personally, it was a cause for celebration rather than consternation.

Yet I did find myself in No Man's Land. As a pastor it's even trickier. Can a pastor rightly officiate communion without acknowledging the miracle of the real presence of Christ to his parishioners? Can a minister in good conscience marry a couple when they do not embrace marriage as a divinely established sacrament? And, knowing that the Eucharist is the matchless centerpiece of Christian worship throughout all ages, can a pastor support a church that rarely serves communion or takes a low view of it? My conclusion was that these issues were so near the epicenter of the Church the apostles founded that it was now my turn to begin my personal sojourn into No Man's Land.

I have heard permutations of this story again and again from ministers and lay people. There may be someone reading this who is in their own private No Man's Land right now. Be encouraged! You are not alone. Many thousands of others have ventured down this ancient path before you, and thousands are following even today. Yes, it can be lonely, because some at your church won't understand why you are asking all the odd questions you are asking. If your family has lingered in the Protestant heritage for generations, you probably won't get much encouragement. And since this is your heritage, you probably also don't have much contact, support, or fellowship with Catholics, either. This will feel, quite literally, like *No Man's Land*. By grace, I understood that this pilgrimage would lead me into lonely places, so I embraced this unique station in life.

It reminded me of times in college when I would go camping by myself. As an Eagle Scout from a scouting family, I enjoyed the outdoors and loved camping. One of my joys during college was to go solo camping. (Please don't tell my mother—it will make her nervous even decades after the fact!) There was a stretch of woods on the banks of Tennessee's Buffalo River that felt like heaven. I would arrive, set up camp, hike and explore during the day, fish for dinner in the afternoon, and enjoy a fire without another soul within miles. I loved that. The solitude and the sound of the water were magical. I once heard an old timer say, "If you are all alone and you don't like the company, you've got yourself a problem." Maybe those solo camping days prepared me for my ecclesiastical No Man's Land. One thing I'm sure of is when a Protestant feels that curious tug and begins to see the Eucharistic majesty, the global beauty, and historical richness of the Catholic Church, he or she is probably going solo camping for a while.

When Saul was converted on the road to Damascus, and took the new name Paul, the book of Acts tells us that shortly after, he made his way to Arabia for about three years. Those are some of Paul's "hidden years," but that time in Arabia was critically important for this servant. Certainly, it was a time of deep reflection, a time of seeking God's will, a time of growth.

In a way, this was Paul's No Man's Land. He was far, far away from Jerusalem and the things familiar to him. This time of detachment and reflection no doubt turned his heart toward God, and allowed him to mature into the Paul we know in the New Testament. His season in Arabia was probably not easy, but it was good. I would be willing to wager that if you asked Paul what was one of the most trying times in his life, he would probably say his time in Arabia. And if you were to ask him about the richest time, he'd also probably say Arabia. During that span of time his life was on hold, things were uncertain, and he was going through momentous personal change. But he was not alone. God was with him, ministering to him, teaching him, and equipping him in ways that would change the world.

There may be someone right now reading this who is experiencing their time in Arabia. I fully understand, I have had my Arabian experience. For weeks, months, a season, even years, you may feel, as Kurt Vonnegut phrased it, like "a man without a country." You are beginning to understand why the former Anglican minister John Henry Cardinal Newman wrote, "To be deep in history is to cease to be Protestant."

Collectively your prayer, study, and reflections have led you to the glorious porch of St. Peter's basilica but not through the door and into full fellowship. For you who are in Arabia, for you who are solo camping on the front porch of St. Peter's, take heart and embrace this season. Yes, it is a time of testing and reflection and challenge. But it might just be one of the riches seasons of growth as God prepares you in a unique way to change the world. Believe me: You are *not* alone.

station fourteen

the nations gather

urant and I decided to go to Italy before our first Easter Vigil and our formal acceptance into the Catholic Church. We'd traveled to Europe before and had visited numerous cathedrals, but this trip was different. Before, when I was a Protestant, cathedrals had seemed beautiful to me, but I always walked away feeling a bit empty. No longer! This is my family, now. This is my Church. One thing I now realize is that the Catholic Church is universal. The Mass we are saying in Memphis is the same one fellow Catholics are saying in Rome, and Japan, and Brazil, and Ireland, and all around the earth. As I worshipped in St. Peter's with people from all over the world, we were all united in one faith, one Eucharist, one family. The Catholic Church isn't perfect, but it is so deep, so rich, so beautiful. If you had told me many years ago that the journey Durant and I were taking together was leading us back home to the Catholic Church, I would not have believed you. But here we are, and what an incredibly rich journey it has been so far. I can say for certainty that it isn't over. In fact, it has really just begun.

Years ago as my wife Sharon and I were approaching our twenty-fifth wedding anniversary, I had the great idea to whisk her away on a romantic anniversary trip to Rome. We would visit the historic sites, see some of the finest art ever created, savor some of the best food in the world, and walk along the Tiber holding hands at night. It didn't happen. Life got in the way—one child needed braces, we moved, another child was entering college, we needed another car…you know the story. It just wasn't our time to go. Holding hands by the Tiber was going to have to wait.

Now, fast forward about five years. As a result of our years of prayer and study, Sharon and I began attending the Rite of Christian Initiation of Adults (RCIA), a program designed to help people explore the Catholic Church. I am very fond of our time in RCIA and will be forever grateful for our wonderful sponsors. I am certain Sharon and I far exceeded the acceptable limit for asking questions! For us this was a rich time of learning, fellowship, self-examination, and prayer. At this point, our experience had led us to the same conclusion reached by Protestant clergyman John Henry Newman, and brilliant writer G.K. Chesterton, and American actor Gary Cooper, and social activist Dorothy Day, and physicist Takashi Nagai, and fantasy writer J.R.R. Tolkien, and French mathematician Joseph Saurin, and Japanese sculptor Etsuro Sotoo, and mega-church Methodist minister Allen Hunt, and German poet Zacharias Werner, and former Presbyterian pastor Scott Hahn, and libertarian economist Thomas Woods, and Olympic figure skater Kim Yu-Na, and tough-guy John Wayne, and British world leader Tony Blair, and atheist physician Alexis Carrel, and author of philosophy Mortimer Adler, and renowned Bostonian professor Peter Kreeft, and political columnist Robert Novak, and jazz pianist and composer Dave Brubeck, all of whom, as adults, consciously embraced Catholicism.

To celebrate this, and to celebrate the conclusion of our productive months in RCIA, Sharon and I planned on going to Rome. This time, it was much more than a trip—it was a pilgrimage. And yes, we finally held hands as we strolled by the Tiber River at night, and enjoyed some of the best food in the world. We also celebrated Mass at the tomb of Leo the Great, and made a first confession before the altar of the Transfiguration at St. Peter's Basilica. We saw the chains that had bound St. Paul during his imprisonment for Christ, and made our way to honor St. Francis by visiting his tomb in Assisi. It was as overwhelming as it was encouraging.

We began to deeply sense our connectedness with Jesus, the apostles and the early Church. In Jerusalem, as we followed in the footsteps of Jesus, and as we by faith walked the much-traveled stations of the Via Dolorosa, we found his footsteps inexorably led us to the Catholic Church. I have intentionally called each chapter of this work a "station" for this reason. Each year as I prayed, researched, and followed my studies, again and again, Sharon and I were continually led to Rome. Now, after years of honest inquiry, we surrendered and acknowledge that these "stations" have indeed led us to Rome, both figuratively and literally.

There was one interesting, and serendipitous twist to our pilgrimage to Rome, an event we could have never foreseen. About two weeks before we were to arrive, Pope Benedict XVI stepped down from the papacy, and we would be in Rome during the conclave, the meeting of the Cardinals from all over the world to select the next Pope. What an amazing field trip before coming into the Church on Easter Vigil! There is no way you can plan this kind of thing.

Sharon and I have a friend who is a priest who at that time was working on his doctoral studies in Rome. He was so gracious, sacrificing a day of his studies to escort us through St. Peter's and around the Vatican. On the day of our tour through the Vatican area, our friend broke it to us that we were not going to be able to see the Sistine Chapel—the Cardinals needed it to select a new Pope! We laughingly deferred.

During our time there, Rome and the Vatican were electrified. A sharply increased security was visible, media towers were going up in St. Peter's Square, priests and cardinals were flooding into Rome along with pilgrims from the four corners of the Earth. We felt a unique buoyancy. For a sojourner who had been in No Man's Land for a number of years, it was a miraculous time to be in the Eternal City.

As the world converged at St. Peter's, the massive plaza flooded with the Church from every nation. The entire plaza, large enough to hold 100,000 to 150,000 pilgrims, is surrounded by our family members, statues of the great saints of history who were joining in this celebration. These saints stood atop a curved colonnade surrounding the vast plaza, intentionally designed by Bernini to resemble the maternal arms of the Church embracing her children. As I looked up toward the face of the basilica, I was struck by the colossal statues of St. Peter and St. Paul, situated as if safe-guarding the Church. Peter is on the left, the Keeper of the Keys, representing his apostolic authority, and Paul stands on the right holding a sword, a symbol of the Word of Truth. While looking at these massive figures I remembered the words of Irenaeus: "We point to the tradition of that very great and very ancient and universally known

Church, which was founded and established at Rome, by the two most glorious Apostles, Peter and Paul."

As I saw these titanic figures surrounded by pilgrims from every corner of the globe, I recalled the words of Clement I, third successor to Peter: "Around these men (Peter and Paul) with their holy lives there are gathered a great throng of the elect." By God's grace I now found myself among that throng. The massive scale of this area at the Vatican almost confounds the mind. It is difficult for the brain to register spaces, perspectives, and objects on that uncommon scale. For the next few days, the Church global would flock to this place. Flags of the world's nations flew, nuns prayed the rosary, the sick converged for healing, youth groups flooded in, people were singing, priests abounded, groups worshipping in ways familiar to them, drums sounded, extended families gathered, groups chanted in unfamiliar languages. There were gestures of universal kindness, sounds of laughter, prayers for the Church, and tears of joy— you would have to have seen it to believe that humans from every walk of life can love and coexist in this way. It was as if the very incense of heaven had wafted through to this world. Every ethnicity, every age group, every form and style of worship, every social class, every artistic expression, all in one spirit, full of joy, coming together in one love—a passionate love for Christ and a passionate love for his Church. I have experienced many things, but hands down, I have never experienced anything like this. It was a reality that will shape my life forever.

To encounter the living God is to be changed. As I looked across this sea of faith, what I witnessed was the divine design, the beauty of one Church, one holy, Catholic, and apostolic church.

Then, looking up, I saw him. Towering over all, standing high upon the crest of St. Peter's Basilica, there he was, ruling over this jubilant throng. It was almost too much to take in, too much to wrap one's mind around, too heavy to process. It was a moment of perfection. Hovering over and looking down upon all of this, was a spectacular statue of Jesus Christ—the Genesis of it all, the King of the Church. In his left hand he holds his cross, the means by which he rescued and ingathered these people to himself. With his right hand he blesses the masses with a loving, outstretched arm. Beneath his feet were the massive doors of his Church, swung open wide for all who desire salvation. There are those exceptional moments on a spiritual pilgrimage when you just can't absorb it all, those holy moments when the goodness of God brings you to your knees. Words fall short, time stops, tears flow, and the Holy Spirit reshapes your life. All you can do is sit in wonder and *be*. This was one of those moments.

I had spent decades studying the Church, had traveled around the earth, had read thousands upon thousands of pages, had spent years in service to the Church, and at St. Peter's in Rome, this is where it all converged, in the deepest places of my heart, with peace like still water. I knew I was finally home. This is my family. This is my Church. This is my home.

The Church coming together at St. Peter's during the Conclave.

A Royal Invitation—
The King Is Knocking

This short text was never intended to be an exhaustive examination of church history, a precise theological document, or an airtight apologetic. In the spirit of my friend St. Irenaeus, the "lover of peace," this work was not intended to prove anybody wrong. The intent of this work is to capture, the best I could, an intimate, personal journey of faith into the Catholic Church, a journey many thousands are currently making and others are quietly considering. Each week, across the world, millions of Christians, representing thousands of Christian sects and denominations, confess that they believe in the "Holy Catholic church." But what does this mean? Do we know what we are confessing?

Before Jesus left this earth, he prayed earnestly to his Father on behalf of his Church. The King prayed for his Kingdom. In this high priestly prayer, our Savior prayed for three things: He prayed for our protection, he prayed that we would love one another, and he prayed that we, his Church, would be one. In 1995 Pope John Paul II wrote the impassioned *Ut Unum Sint, (That They All May Be One)*. This work reminds us that our call to unity is a serious Christian obligation—not an ancillary undertaking nor a tertiary endeavor. It stands at the core of what it means to follow Jesus Christ. It is an expression of faith as central as feeding the poor, loving our neighbor, and attending to the means of grace. Within this noteworthy text, John Paul wrote, "I thank the Lord that he has led us to make progress along the path of unity and communion between Christians, a path difficult but so full of joy." Our efforts toward unity are indeed challenging, yet this honorable vocation, this calling, is also a great joy—a joy to bring honor to Christ and a joy to serve his Church. It is our calling, it is our vocation, to be one Church.

To my Protestant brothers and sisters, whom I love, all I would encourage you to do is to have an open heart and an open mind on your pilgrimage toward heaven. If you have ever wondered whether there were more—more to worship, more to the Church, more to being part of a universal family, more to service, more to the Eucharist—there *is* more. Look to the ancient paths. If that hunch has been tugging at you for some time that we were created for more, let me suggest that you continue on your personal pilgrimage. Continue reading, continue searching, continue praying, continue asking a lot of questions, and continue to fulfill your calling to be one. We are all on a journey. We are each on a pilgrimage. Let me encourage you as fellow sojourners, just as other people of goodwill encouraged me: Keep growing, keep searching, keep knocking at the door of truth, because as my wise and ever-patient father used to say in the face of mystery, "You just never know."

Today, two thousand years after Jesus prayed his high priestly prayer, there are sadly an astonishing *thirty thousand* denominations scattered throughout the world espousing every kind of doctrine, teaching, and belief. Often when difficulties arise, rather than humbly striving toward unity, difficulty and dissent lead to the formation of yet another denomination, and then another, and yet another. Presently, we are not one. We have not embraced our vocation toward unity. His sheep are not one. Our Good Shepherd desires unity, one body, one family, one Church. Far too idealistic? True, faith often appears impractical, even impossible at times in the face of overwhelming difficulty, yet Jesus Christ, the King of Glory, has lovingly asked his Church to be one.

The issue is not about the size of the task. This issue is about the authority of the One speaking. In obedience to his Word and for his majesty, we are to be relentlessly and selflessly striving toward unity—one Church, one, holy, Catholic, and apostolic Church. Remember, nothing is impossible with God. Jesus said to his Church, "Behold I stand at the door and knock." His knocking is an invitation, an invitation to come home, an invitation to be one.

Epilogue—The New Evangelization

The other day, I saw a bumper sticker that read, "Catholic and proud!" I'd never seen one of these before. As simple as this bumper sticker may be, it represents a much larger movement in the history of the Church. Currently there is an encouraging new enthusiasm, a new wind blowing through the Catholic Church. I could sense this positivism during the life and ministry of John Paul II and on to this very day through works such as those of Fr. Robert Barron of Chicago in his visually stunning and intellectually engaging DVD series entitled *Catholicism*.

In an exciting way, the Catholic Church is reaching out, opening its doors to the nations. Another example of this renewal of zeal: the extraordinary increase of Catholic young people. Recently in Brazil, millions of eager young people gathered for World Youth Day to celebrate their Catholic faith. Presently across America, through RCIA, friends are inviting friends to honestly explore the Catholic Church. The Dynamic Catholic Book Program is invigorating and equipping tens of thousands of Catholics across the country, and the enrollment of Catholic seminaries are the highest that they have been in the United States in a quarter of a century. The Catholic Church in a fresh way is earnestly inviting millions of believers home. This is an exciting time for the Church, as there is a renewed interest in worship, Bible study, apologetics, missions, service ministries, and global outreach.

More and more Catholics are studying in order to truly understand their Catholic identity and to celebrate their great heritage. This is a work of the Holy Spirit and the Church is in a wonderful season of growth. If my studies have taught me anything, they have taught me that my story is only one of thousands upon thousands among believers from all over the earth who are making their way back to the Catholic Church. If you have found this text to be encouraging or helpful in some way, join the New Evangelization and pass it along to a friend or loved one. This tiny gesture may actually play a part of this global movement as God gathers a people to himself.

Peace and blessings to you.

T. Durant Fleming

.

Prayer of St. Leopold

O God, source of life and love, you gave St. Leopold a tremendous compassion
for sinners and a desire for church unity. Through his prayers,
grant that we may acknowledge our need for forgiveness,
show love to others, and strive to bring about a living unity among Christians,
through our Lord Jesus Christ, who lives and reigns forever and ever. Amen.

Helpful Sources

Barron, Robert E. *Catholicism: A Journey to the Heart of the Faith*. Crown Publishing Group, New York, 2011.

Catholic Church. *Catechism of the Catholic Church*. 2nd ed. Vatican: Libreria Editrice Vaticana, 2000.

EWTN Journey Home. "Former Presbyterian - Marcus Grodi with Dr. David Anders." Online video clip. YouTube, 8 February, 2010.

Gibbons, James. *Faith of Our Fathers*, Kessinger Publishing, Whitefish, Montana, 2003.

Gonzalez, Justo. *The Story of Christianity: The Early Church to the Present Day*. Harper Collins Publishers, 1984.

Hahn, Scott and Kimberly. *Rome Sweet Home*. Ignatius Press, San Francisco, 1993.

Hahn, Scott. *Signs of Life: 40 Catholic Customs and Their Biblical Roots*. Doubleday, New York, 2009.

Paul II. Encyclical Letter. *Ut Unum Sint*. 25 May, 1995.

Kelly, Matthew. *Rediscover Catholicism: A Spiritual Guide to Living with Passion and Purpose*. Beacon Publishing, 2010.

Kreeft, Peter. "Dr. Peter Kreeft's Conversion to Catholicism from Protestantism (Full)." Online video clip. YouTube, 27 January, 2013.

The Catholic Café Christian Radio Show and Catholic Podcast. Host Deacon Jeff Drzycimski (in his "luxurious corner booth") with his ever-affable co-host Tom Dorian. www.catholic café.com. 11 August, 2013.

The New American Bible. Wichita, Kansas, Fireside Catholic Publishers, 1987.

"Catholicism addresses the deepest longings of the human heart. It fosters a mystagogical imagination which ponders things seen and the unseen, taps into the liturgical rhythm of heaven, and boldly encourages tasting the goodness of God."

— T.D.F.

Visiting St. Peter's Basilica, Vatican City.